THE COMPLETE VERSION

175
SMALL BUSINESS
TIPS TO LIVE BY

BATTLE-TESTED ADVICE TO HELP
SMALL BUSINESSES, START-UPS, &
ENTREPRENEURS SURVIVE AND THRIVE

STUART GOLDSTEIN, MBA

CEO, GOLDART CONSULTING LLC
SMALL BUSINESS SPECIALISTS

WHAT'S INSIDE HERE

In this book, there are 4 independent sections totaling 150 Tips with over 40 Tips in each section.

1. Financial Management
2. Marketing and Sales
3. Strategy and Planning
4. Management and Execution

Financial Management (Page 5)

- Topics Include: Business Plans, Cash Management, Pricing Elements, Investments and Equity Raising, Debt Management, Negotiating, Financial Analysis etc.

Marketing and Sales (Page 49)

- Topics Include: Targeting, Advertising, Messaging, Sales Management, Customer Relationships, Marketing Spend, Elements Mix, Marketing Strategy, Specialization, etc.

Strategy and Planning (Page 95)

- Topics Include: Competition Strategy, An Integrated Path to Success, Corporate Credibility, Position Defense, Change Management, Client Approach, etc.

Management and Execution (Page 137)

- Topics Include: Visionary Makeup, Executive Stability, Time and Corporate Management, Partnerships, Most Important Words, Executive Skills, Employee Approaches, etc.

Goldart Consulting LLC
(888) 203 - 6419
stuartg@goldartconsulting.com
www.goldartconsulting.com

ABOUT THE AUTHOR

Mr. Goldstein is currently the President and Founder of Goldart Consulting LLC, a Small Business consulting firm specializing in marketing, finance, strategy & management consulting to micro and small businesses, start-up operation. Current and past clients are based throughout America, as well as in many countries in Europe and Asia. He has helped Small Businesses generate many millions in revenue and profits.

Previously, as the Director of Financial Planning and Analysis at SFX Entertainment Inc., a forerunner to Live Nation Inc., Mr. Goldstein helped analyze and complete over $3 billion in Merger and Acquisition activity including the acquisition of the industry's leading concert promoters and entertainment companies such as Bill Graham Presents, PACE Entertainment, Contemporary Productions, Don Law, & David Falk Mgmt.

Prior to this, Mr. Goldstein was the Manager of Strategic Planning in Corporate Sales and Marketing at Cablevision Systems, then the country's fifth largest cable system and owner of several Entertainment assets including the Madison Square Garden, Radio City Music Hall, the New York Knicks and Rangers, and the American Movie Classics and Bravo television channels.

Mr. Goldstein has a Masters of Business Administration in Finance from New York University and a Bachelor of Science in Management in Marketing from Tulane University in New Orleans.

INTRODUCTION:
CASSANDRA &
HOW THIS CAME TO BE

I started these Tips a long time ago as I noticed over my years of consulting I'd say the same things to many different clients. My goal in formalizing it was to help new business entrepreneurs avoid the mistakes and pitfalls that I saw in my previous career and experiences with clients.

Over the years I've added to the list, expanded it, refined it to ensure each Tip captures the essential. I've chosen the short form as attention is limited and wisdom is brevity. They are short shots of knowledge and experience that hopefully educate, enlighten, remind and spark interest.

I have always found entrepreneurs to be beautiful things. Sometimes they don't have beautiful characters, but Entrepreneurs are amazing, people who leap, jump in and risk, often without the knowledge or experience, but always with a wonderful dream. I find that magical, and courageous, worthy of praise and admiration.

To those people this book is dedicated, and to all those who have and who are considering the leap, I wish you the greatest success. May the jump bring you everything you are hoping for and may this book be a useful tool in your arsenal.

I named my consulting company many years ago as I was starting out with an anagram of sorts using the first four letters of my last name and the last three letters of my first name. Many years later, after working in the trenches for more than a decade, I came across the new name I would use to start another company with a similar objective, helping Small Businesses. I would call it Cassandra Consulting.

Cassandra comes from Greek mythology. The story goes she either slept with someone she shouldn't have or didn't sleep with someone she should, and for this, she was cursed with gift of foresight. The ability to know what is going to happen before it does. The curse? No one was to believe her.

There is poor Cassandra in Shakespeare's Troilus and Cressida telling the Trojan Men not to let the gift horse into the gates of Troy. She pleads with them, It's full of soldiers!   Quiet Cassandra, the leaders say. No one listens.

I've been doing Small Business consulting for 22 years now and my appreciation for Cassandra grows with the years. What follows is a pre-emptive attempt to help Small Businesses avoid troubles before, during and after the start of their new venture. And to help them succeed over the long term in the turbulent water of entrepreneurship.

FINANCIAL MANAGEMENT

Financial Management are core activities that owners/entrepreneurs undertake to preserve business interests. They include, among other initiatives, managing accounting, creating and analyzing budgets / forecasts, directing cash flow through Receivable & Payable efforts and completing financial statement analysis.

They lead to important decisions taken that effect the funding and sustainability of the business, and its capacity to achieve its goals in other critical areas of the enterprise. Further, it includes the area of investments into the company and investments the company make in outside ventures.

Often known as Merger and Acquisitions (M&A) and Sale & Purchase decisions, these are essential financial areas that can ultimately discern the value of a company's worth and how the entrepreneur is able to capture that value personally.

1.

"REMEMBER: CASH IS MORE IMPORTANT THAN YOUR MOTHER."

Cash is both the blood and oxygen of a business. Without it, you're out of business. Period. Full stop.

So always know how much you have, how much you'll need soon, and how much you'll need in the future. Forecasting is key in detailed plans and schedules.

Also husband it by managing your payments and collections judiciously. Always try to negotiate better payment terms, from clients regarding invoices, and suppliers regarding deliveries.

2.

"REVIEW THE CASH & SALES EVERY NEW MORNING."

This is a habit that everyone needs to establish in their business life. The first thing every business owner should do every morning is review their sales from the day before and check their cash balance in the bank account. Every morning. First thing. Even if you're just beginning.

This puts your focus on where it needs to be: Sales and cash. Because when we take care of these, good things follow.

So check your bank balance, total sales, credit card and cash receipts every morning. Keep a monthly running tally in a spreadsheet.

3.

"YOUR COSTS ARE ALWAYS THE FIRST BASIS OF YOUR PRICE."

Coming up with your price is often difficult. Many factors play into the final price. But the first basis is your variable costs and the margin desired.

So complete a thorough cost analysis of what you want to sell. Raw materials, service fees, commissions, insurance costs, delivery costs etc. Make sure to capture all of your variable costs, those that vary with an additional increment of sales.

If you can't cover your variable costs, stop selling it. This is not a loss leader, it's just a loss and that's the quickest route to bankruptcy.

4.

"ANALYZE DECISIONS FINANCIALLY BEFORE YOU DECIDE."

This applies to all areas of a Small Business, not just the Finance decisions. All decisions have a financial impact, and if you are not analyzing the potential impact prior to making them, you are not putting in the appropriate thought levels.

Budgets, forecasts, planning are not unnecessary homework or time-wasting assignments. They are the strategic analyses that lead to better decisions and better future outcomes. So do the work beforehand. You'll save time, money and perhaps your company in the long run.

5.

"KNOW YOUR NUMBERS BETTER!"

Gross Margin, Break-even, Free Cash, Debt to equity, expense as a percentage of revenue, etc.

The answers are here. The present and the future are written in these numbers of your business that tell you the picture of the past and the current, and what may be supported in the future

Understand what these numbers are telling you about the solvency, the potential operating leverage and profitability, and cash generating capacities of your business. And comprehend how they should influence your strategic business decisions. This is where a better accounting system is a must.

6.

"BE VERY CONSERVATIVE WHEN MAKING PROJECTIONS."

It has been my experience that almost all projections I see are too optimistic. And usually, it's not even close which ends up being embarrassing and credibility crushing.

Sales, customer retention, profitability, cash flow. All of them overestimate the business's ability to achieve.

Recognize that it is human nature to be overly optimistic, and run your models on severely-reduced figures. Reduce your forecasts, then reduce them again. If your business model still works, you'll have more confidence that your results will resemble reality in the end.

7.

"DON'T SPEND MONEY YOU HAVEN'T RECEIVED."

Some many things happen between a cash provider saying Yes, and you receiving your money. Be it investments, sales, refunds or deposits, it is shocking how many times they become illusionary *after* the Yes. Next days become next week, next week becomes next month. And next month often never comes about.

But people spend these funds irrespective of whether they've been received. The end result is late fees, bounced checks, finance charges, and all sorts of upset providers. So spend the money only when you see it in your bank balance, not before.

8.

"LEARN FROM BOOKKEEPING SOFTWARE."

Whether it's Quickbooks, Freshbooks or another product, use bookkeeping software and do the books yourself! *Because success comes from knowledge implemented.*

If you don't have a financial background, this process will be an invaluable education. Even if you have financial know-how, doing your own bookkeeping will have you more closely watching the elements effecting your business.

So many people outsource this to accountants and never review it, let alone understand it. I suggest that each month you input, reconcile, print up, review and analyze your monthly reports yourself.

13

9.

"FOCUS ON MARGIN AND PROFITABILITY."

Sales are great, we love sales. But sales don't feed your family. Gross margin does. Profitability does.

People get so excited about making sales without realizing that Sales without an appropriate gross margin leads to a money-losing operation. So many companies, public and private eventually have to stop operations because though they had sales, they did not have gross margin sufficient to cover the costs of the business.

Keep your focus on the right prizes: Gross Margin, Operating Cash flow and Net Income. Since cash is king, these metrics tell the real story.

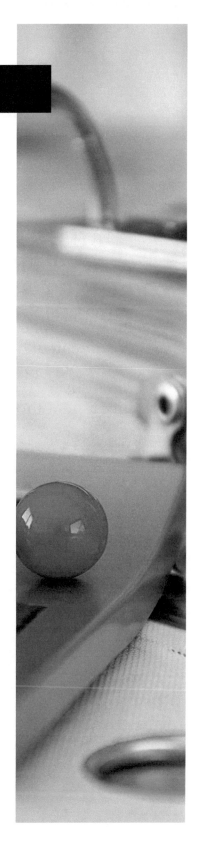

10.

"BUSINESS PLANS ARE FIRST AN INTERNAL ANALYSIS OF A PROJECT'S CHANCE FOR SUCCESS."

Business plans should start as an internal document, an analysis for the prospective business owner only to see if this business idea is worth the time, heartache, and most importantly, money investment they're about to make.

Note the usage of "prospective." It's because you do the business plan before you start the business.

After an assessment is made, through a thorough business analysis, that the idea has a reasonable chance of working, then they can become an External document, a communication vehicle to outside parties such as banks and investors.

11.

"CALCULATE YOUR FINANCIAL RATIOS EVERY QUARTER."

Or even every month if needed at critical periods of the business life cycle!

Please research Coverage Ratios, Leverage ratios and Equity Ratios. These calculations derive from financial results, and communicate information about the health, investability and sustainability of your business.

Investors and bankers will make their lending / investing decisions partially based on an analysis of these calculations. It is essential that owners are versed in them and are competent to talk about their calculations and implications.

12.

"ALWAYS DO BOTTOM-UP BUSINESS PLANS."

I can tell every time I see a business plan that was built from the Top down (numbers chosen from out of the air). The sales figures all round out neatly and the growth fits a simple trajectory. And like Monopoly money, they're not worth the paper they're printed on. Yet people do this, choosing a revenue number then backing into it. Useless.

But bottom-up financial schedules, those that detail specific prices, take rates, volumes sold etc. generate useful schedules that can better reflect possible outcomes and produce forecasts that are believable, perhaps actionable.

13.

"CALCULATE GROSS MARGIN WITH ALL EXPENSES THAT VARY WITH A UNIT OF REVENUE."

One thing a Gross Margin analysis shows us is how much of each dollar of revenue we receive, we keep to pay our fixed expenses. The higher the margin, either in percentage or absolute dollars, the more left over to get us towards profitability.

But the analysis must include everything that varies with each unit of revenue sold. Too often people leave out expenses that are substantial, but not directly related to the production of the revenue. In other words, don't forget things like commissions, sales taxes, shipping, etc.

14.

"RAISING BAD CAPITAL HAS AN EXISTENTIAL EFFECT ON YOUR BUSINESS."

Another rule herein says it all: Get the right deal, not just any deal. Regardless of the type of funding desired, it is important to understand there is such a thing as "bad money."

Sometimes the deal isn't good because investors want too much, sometimes the lender is unscrupulous. Sometimes, there is not just not a good fit / match between the two sides.

Don't take the money no matter how desperate. All you're doing is exchanging one battle for another, and things don't just work out later. The headaches and heartaches to come are not worth it.

15.

"BUSINESS PLAN PROGRAMS FOUND ONLINE SUCK."

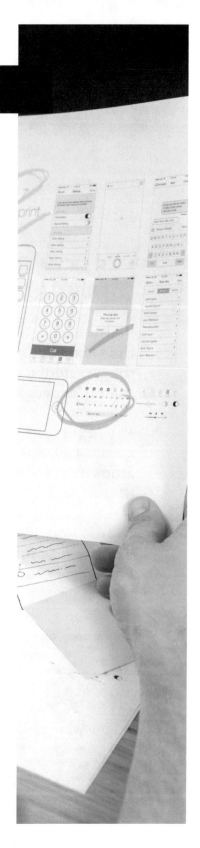

They are worthless. One-size fits all, ask-you-simple questions, give-only-simple answers wastes of time / money.

No two businesses are exactly alike, and it's in the specificity of your idea and your situation that will make the difference to lenders and investors.

Your business, your time and money investment, is riding on the analysis you complete. Your next two-five years, and perhaps your life savings, that's what's on the line. And you're leaving it to some free software you found on the internet?

C'mon, you can do better.

20

16.

"WHEN TIMES DEMAND SLOW PAYING, MAKE SURE EVERYBODY GETS SOME."

Many Small Businesses have tough periods, ones that lead to them rationing cash and slow paying their vendors. It happens more times to businesses than is expected. In fact, it's quite common.

Pay everyone vendor you owe money to *some* amount of money. To less important, pay the least amount respectful, and of course, pay your most important vendors more.

Even a small payment says, "Thank you. We know we owe you, we haven't forgotten, we aren't ignoring you." It will buy you more future patience.

17.

"DEBT SHOULD BE A PART OF CAPITAL STRUCTURE... BUT BEWARE."

I believe that every Small Business should have some debt in their capital structure, be it bank or personal loans, government Small Business loans (SBA), or even credit cards. Having debt allows you to leverage assets without giving up equity in your company.

While debt isn't to be feared, it is to be managed actively as it very often is the road to ruin. When interest and principal payments become too onerous on cash, serious problems arise, Ratios such as Coverage and Debt to Equity need to be analyzed for signs of trouble.

18.

"REVIEW AN ACTION *IN DEPTH* AFTER IT IS TAKEN AND THE RESULTS ARE IN!"

Better decision-making results from learning from past wins and losses. Yet so many people take an action, see the results of the action, then move on to the next things without really digging into what happened, and more importantly, *why!* did what happen....happen.

Success is a practiced art so we need to analyze results, question and find answers within the results, and then form strategy based on those analyses completed.

Make your business efforts intellectual. It'll keep you challenged and invested.

19.

"FIXED EXPENSES ARE THE DEATH OF A STARTING BUSINESS."

Sometimes referred to as the catch-all term of, "Overhead," but either way, unnecessarily high Fixed Expenses, those expenses that do not vary with an additional unit sold of Revenue, put a severe financial strain on a business, making it difficult to survive in the beginning of the endeavor.

Like a Terminator coming after you every month, Fixed expenses have to be managed to the lowest level possible. This includes Salaries, Benefits, Rent, Insurance, and Utilities (Telephone and Energy). Negotiating variable rates, usage-based programs, and revenue commission structures can help greatly.

20.

"EQUITY IS LIMITED: TREAT IT AS A MOST PRECIOUS THING."

There is only 100% of your company so you can't make more or sell more (unless you're Zero Mostel). So one needs to treat shares in their company as a most valuable item when early investors come calling or employees want equity.

There is most certainly a time and place to give and sell equity, and ways to do it right with time vesting and success-based compensation. And certainly selling shares is integral to growth and success

But one must be judicious in these decisions. Go slowly to ensure proper valuation, the fit with new partners, and enough room yet managing control.

21.

"KNOW THE DIFFERENCE BETWEEN RETURN *OF* INVESTMENT & RETUN *ON* INVESTMENT."

Clients say to me, "I got my money back" without realizing that just getting your money back on a project or investment is a fail.

If you just get the return of your investment back you lost time and money because we must always take into account *Opportunity cost*. The time and money you spent on this thing prohibited you from spending on another thing that could have gotten you a return *on* your investment.

You want a multiple on both of your investments, time and money. Anything less than 3x is insufficient. So analyze deals and projects with this mindset.

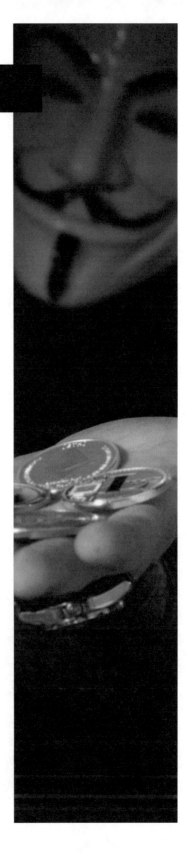

22.

"TIME & DELAYS
KILL DEALS."

Especially in Finance deals (sales or purchases of companies, capital investments, bank loans etc.) the longer a deal goes without closing, the less of a chance that it will ever close. Succinctly said, Time kills deals.

So it is incumbent on the Small Business owner to drive forward the elements they can control, and even the ones they can't towards completion.

Pushing for the meetings and the response and the analyses and all other efforts that bring a deal to fruition must be marshalled understanding that the sands hourglass are filtering away.

23.

"RAISE MONEY WHEN YOU DON'T NEED IT."

There's an old rule that stands up over time: You can never have too much cash.

And so few are going to step up and offer your money when you're desperate for it. And if they do, the terms they will offer you will be brutal as they have all the leverage, be they lenders or investors.

So it is so important to raise money when you don't need it...so it's there for when you do. Look for opportunities to expand credit lines or take on investors when things are solid as a fair rate is more possible to achieve, and you will be ready to weather the rainy day.

24.

"YOU ONLY GET ONE SHOT AT AN INVESTOR."

It's important for Entrepreneurs looking to raise capital to know that potential investors (White Knights, Venture Capital, Private Equity) are bombarded every day with other businesses searching for capital. In 100 years, they can't get to all of them given their limited time, let alone investment capital.

So you get one shot and you can't blow it. So all the pre-work needs to be done. The presentation must be clear and concise to a fault, and you must know your numbers and your field/industry inside and out.

This isn't Tinder. Never go out looking for investment capital until you are fully ready.

25.

"BUILD FINANCIAL CUSHIONS INTO PROJECT ANALYSES."

Especially with financing projects, but even so with anything budget-related, build a cushion into your forecasts. Because surprises with expenses are deadly to businesses so at a minimum one must account for the risk with a cushion.

When I make budgets and forecasts, I add at least a 10% and sometimes 15% or even 20% cushion into each item. This is to ensure I've captured all that is need to bring the project to fruition. If I'm wrong and the actual is lowered, happy day, the lack of expense falls to the bottom line.

But our job as managers is to reduce risk and over-optimism is killer of business dreams.

26.

"UNDERSTAND THE THREE MAIN FINANCIAL STATEMENTS."

There are three main financial statements that all businesses, from the corner store to Apple Computer, are analyzed by.

1. Income Statement
(otherwise known as a Profit & Loss Statement, or colloquially, P&L)

2. Balance Sheet

3. Cash Flow Analysis

Each of these statements communicates and explains various different information on the state of the company they are related to.

You don't need to be a financial analyst, but it is essential that Small Business people have a good working understanding of each statement.

31

27.

"MAIN FINANCIAL STATEMENT: INCOME STATEMENT"

It's otherwise known interchangeably as a Profit & Loss Statement, or colloquially, P&L. As the second name implies, this statement is a graphic explanation of the profitability of the company. Or loss if the case may be.

The statement outlines a basic formula: Revenue minus expenses with the result being profit or loss.

The main categories always calculated and shown are Revenue, Gross Margin, some calculation of expenses be it Fixed and Variable, COGS or Selling, General & Administisitrative (SG&A) and finally a meausre of profitability.

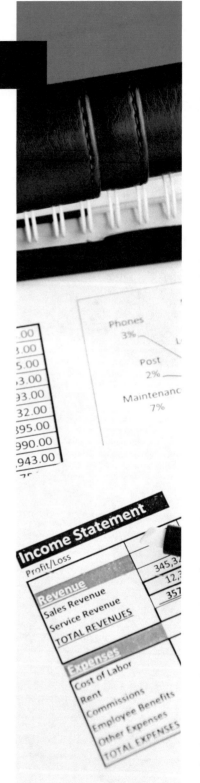

28.

"MAIN FINANCIAL STATEMENT: THE BALANCE SHEET"

The Balance Sheet is a personal net worth statement, but for a business. It's really a simple formula: Assets minus Liabilities equals Owner's Equity.

An asset is something that has value. The main assets in a Small Business are typically Cash, Accounts Receivable, Inventory, Property Plant and Equipment.

A liability is amount that is owed to other. The main liabilities typically in a Small Business are Accounts Payable, Loans Payable,

Owner's Equity, which is the difference between the two above, represents a measure of value of the business.

Apr	M
2500	
8000	
4000	

29.

"MAIN FINANCIAL STATEMENT: CASH FLOW ANALYSIS"

The least well-known of the main financial statements, but in some ways the most important, is the Cash Flow Statement which tracks Cash specifically (see Tip #1 in this book!).

In general, there are three ways Businesses generate cash. One is from its operations, the second is from investments made in assets outside the company, the third is cash from investments made by outsiders into the company.

This schedule tracks the net effect, so positive or negative, of each driver of cash in the business. Just the fact that this analysis and is one of the main schedules completed for all business underscores how important cash is to businesses.

5% of total

30.

"KNOW THE DIFFERENCE BETWEEN AN INVESTOR AND A PARTNER."

The most substantial factors playing into the difference between an investor and a partner tend to be a. ownership percentage, b. corporate control and c. levels of input in day-to-day operations.

When looking to raise capital, the entrepreneur must consider the investor in terms of the three elements. How much input do you want? What control will they have over decision making? Understand that the higher the equity, the more rights an investor has and the more input, control they're entitled to.

Make sure you've thought it through because miscalculating can be very painful in the long run.

31.

"IT'S NOT WHAT YOU GET....BUT IT IS WHAT YOU KEEP."

This note is about the importance of taxes and a business strategy to maximize after-tax cash flow. That is, the money that remains either in the business or in the pockets of the owners after taxes have been paid on profitability.

There are many decisions that can effect after-tax cash flow. For example, when you make investments in inventory or fixed expenses. Another is when you pay off outstanding bills and accounts receivables. A third may be the declaring of certain revenues.

Talk to your accountant, to understand more the decisions and the timing, *especially* at your end

32.

"KNOW YOUR BURN RATE."

As I said in the first tip in this book, Cash is more important than your mother. When we are out of cash, and out of external lines to draw on cash, we are essentially out of business. So we track cash as we would track our blood and oxygen.

A burn rate is the rate at which a company is losing Net Cash on a monthly basis. If you are net losing $5,000 in cash every month and your cash balance is only $30,000 than you only have six months of cash on hand before catastrophe.

So calculate your Burn Rate based on the past six months of net cash production or deficit. It is a countdown clock that cannot be ignored, and must be managed to protect your future.

33.

"USE CASH ACCOUNTING PROCEDURES, NOT ACRUAL."

This gets a little deeper into accounting, but it's a decision to make right at the top when it comes to bookkeeping so it's important.

Cash Accounting is simply measuring activities when they affect the cash balance. Accrual accounting is measuring activities when they occur. Make a sale in September but don't receive money until December, Cash accounting books that in December. Accrual accounting accounts for it in September. The same thing with expenses.

Cash accounting is easier to understand, manage and analyze on a recurring basis. Just cash in and cash out, nothing more fancy than that. It's better for the uninitiated and the new venture.

34.

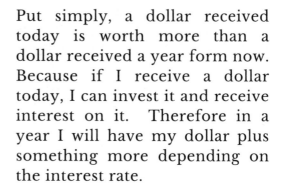

"REMEMBER THE TIME VALUE OF MONEY."

Put simply, a dollar received today is worth more than a dollar received a year form now. Because if I receive a dollar today, I can invest it and receive interest on it. Therefore in a year I will have my dollar plus something more depending on the interest rate.

In business though even more options exist. A dollar received today can do so many more things. It can be invested in high ROI projects, it can be used to pay down high rate credit card debts, it can increase my credit rating.

So when discussing terms with both vendors and customers, remember the maxim of the time value of money and make decisions accordingly.

35.

"TAKE ADVANTAGE OR EVEN SUGGEST PAYMENT TERMS."

Payment terms is when a vender offers you a discount on the total cost of your invoice when you pay your bill in a certain defined time frame. They come in various different shapes and sizes, but a very common example is known as 2/10 net 30.

In this example, the purchaser is rewarding you by paying off a bill quickly, here receiving a 2% discount by paying the invoice in 10 days. This is one example, nothing is a hard, fast rule or law.

So if a vender does not offer them, go ahead and suggest one yourself. Develop a plan that works for you and present it to the vender. Remember you're probably not the only one is cash strapped.

36.

"ENSURE A PROPER RISK-RETURN ON PROJECTS AND INVESTMENTS."

It is a maxim in business that when we take on more risk, we are doing it to receive a greater return. In business we talk of a Hurdle rate, essentially the minimum return we need to achieve on a product we think of something as a good investment. These rates vary from company to company based generally on their borrowing rate or their cost of capital.

Regardless of the calculation of that, it's important to understand that when we take on risk, usually defined as usage of our precious cash, we are getting rewarded for it. And the greater the investment, which means the greater the risk, we better make sure the potential upside in return is there if everything succeeds. Otherwise wait, save your cash.

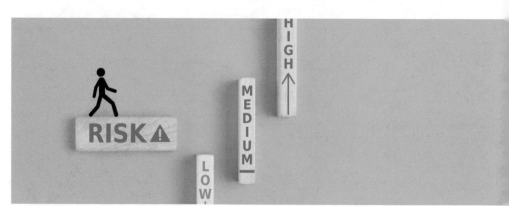

37.

"MAKE CORRECT INVESTMENTS IN BUSINESS INSURANCE."

I think it was Socrates who originally said, "Shit happens." In Small Businesses, it tends to happen early and often. Insurance is one of those things you think you don't need until something happens and you desperately need it to save your business. Don't wait for that moment because it'll be too late. Buy Business insurance appropriate to your line of business.

Business insurance comes in different forms covering different things. Often stores should have liability insurance to protect against accidents in store. Other businesses need Officers and Directors insurance in case a company is sued for things it said or promised. A legitimate lawsuit, an even illegitimate ones, can destroy years of work in a moment's notice.

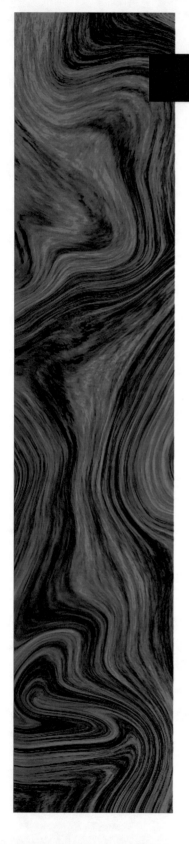

38.

"TRACK LIQUIDITY."

In Business, liquidity is defined as the ability to turn assets into usable cash. Obviously then the most liquid asset is actual cash. On the other end of the scale there are assets that are very illiquid, ie., difficult to turn into cash, like buildings owned. Generally it will take very long time to turn a building into usable cash.

Other assets such as Accounts Receivable and Inventory are non-cash assets that have shorter transitions into cash than let's say large plant equipment.

Businesses want to track liquidity by calculating very liquid assets plus various borrowing lines like credit cards or a credit line at a lender to understand the full cash available potential of a company. A sharp reduction in liquidity is generally a sign of financial stress and needs to be watched carefully.

39.

"WHEREVER POSSIBLE, EXTEND PAYMENTS."

The fine art of cash management for New and Small Businesses is very often about getting your suppliers / vendors to allow you to extend payments to a future date when hopefully your business will have greater cashflow. While being in the state of needing extensions is far from optimal, the ability to get payment extensions can be life saving for a business.

I have found honesty and a date-specific payment plan are often the best tools at your disposal for convincing vendors to take the risk on you. But note: There are risks to asking for payment extensions as it tells the counterparty that your business is not in good financial shape which may affect their willingness to work with you. But in general, if managed well with all debts ultimately paid, it's worth it.

44

40.

"UNDERTAKE YEAR-END TAX DECISIONS AND ACTIVITIES "

There are certain decisions and steps almost all Small Businesses should take at the end of each year to ensure better financial conditions in the coming year. This largely revolves around tax policies, and where possible, spending on certain investments that will reduce profitability in the current year so that ultimately less taxes are paid.

For example, if one is able to prepay certain expenses in December, the business will be less profitable on an income basis, which will necessitate lower tax payments come April. As always, do your research, and if possible, speak with your accountant to devise appropriate and legal planning that is most beneficial.

41.

"ANALYZE MARKETING AVERAGES: AVERAGE REVENUE & MARGIN PER SALE FIGURES."

While this Tip could fit in both Finance and Marketing sections, it's the Finance people who'll do it.

Track Average Revenue and Average Margin per sale to see if progress is being made in creating effective marketing campaigns and enhancing the operating leverage. Ideally, both of these metrics are increasing over time as the company becomes more efficient and effective in its operations, be they marketing or production. But too many Small Business don't review these metrics even though they're easy to calculate: Divide the Total Revenue or Margin by the number of sales completed. Simple.

A CORP.
AL BALANCE Su
($ 000's)

ent %	1-30 days %	31-60
40.4	2343	34.4	685
36.8	1922	34.9	1432
38.2	1668	31.4	1171
50.8	955	12.2	819
42.5	1672	22.8	460
33.7	1982	32.1	945
45.1	948	32.6	1210
34.6	2054	24.1	456
31.0	1664	24.0	1135
27.6	1241	18.7	818
32.1	1722	27.2	604
24.3	1471	24.8	923
24.0	837	23.5	580
25.0	928	25.6	546
30.9	917	23.4	527
26.0	1052	28.1	568
28.2	941	21.6	689
21.4	1602	24.8	844
25.6	939	14.2	1271
24.5	1067	27	1015
26.6	1140	23.4	7
34.3	1205	23.0	
28.8	1536	28.0	
24.8	1604	27.4	4
57.3	3180		1265
34.0	2850		1978
36.5	2586	0	1698
42.7	20	17.6	1387

42.

"DEVELOP ACCOUNTS RECEIVABLE POLICY."

Certainly we're tracking our accounts receivables and watching our aging schedule, right? Reviewing it monthly, right?

The next step is developing the company policy about accounts receivable and what happens when clients don't pay their bills. Many questions arise about what to do when clients don't pay their bills. Do we cut them off from additional ordering? Do we demand upfront payment going forward? Do we remand the case to an attorney or a bad debt firm to pursue legal remedies to try to recoup a portion of the money owed?

All of this varies by industry, by company size, and even by company situation, like cash flush or desperation. The key is make policy, implement it, and be very clear with late payers.

47

43.

"DON'T BOTHER WITH PROJECTIONS MORE THAN THREE YEARS."

Some things aren't worth the paper they're printed on, and projections for more than three years from today are one of them. However, many times, you will be asked to produce five and even ten-year projections for banks and investors. Don't let it be a time-waster.

The simple truth of the matter is that no one can forecast anything meaningfully that much time in advance. Too many things change including products and markets, business models and also economic realities. Completing this task isn't worth your time. And if you are absolutely forced to complete them, get it over as quickly, with his little effort as possible because the one thing is for sure: they will be so wrong.

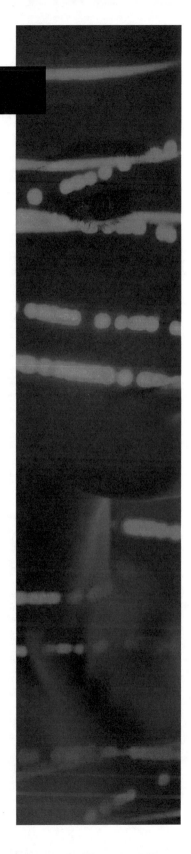

MARKETING AND SALES

A broad definition of Marketing is all activities that a business undertakes to have its current and potential customer bases to exhibit a certain behavior. Sometimes that behavior is an action, like moving a client to buying our product. Other times, it's a behavior like a customer feeling certain ways about our company. Altogether, Marketing is about taking actions to affect behaviors and sales is a subset area of Marketing, usually the most important element under the rubric.

Said another way, we undertake marketing to drive Sales and Brand equity, the value that our market place on our brand. The tools for achieving Marketing are almost endless when we define the term this way.

But most classically, they tend to fall into two broad categories. Traditional tools such as advertising, public relations and promotions and newer modern tools that have almost become dominant in the last 15 years. Internet advertising, SEO development, Instagram and YouTube videos, Tiktok etc.

1.

"REMEMBER! YOUR BRAND IS MORE IMPORTANT THAN YOUR SIBLINGS."

The Brand should ALWAYS stand for everything your business is and hopes to be. Everything reflects on your brand from customer service to product quality and offerings to your messaging and prices. You need to be constantly be asking yourself, "How does this affect my brand?"

Since it's the whole ball game, it's important to know how to build one effectively, how to craft each element into a singular whole that communicates with one united message. Take all the time this needs, it's that essential.

2.

"KNOW THE FOUR PS OF MARKETING."

Price.
Product.
Placement.
Promotion.

These are the levers of marketing at every business's disposal. There are more complicated schemes to describe the elements of marketing, but I find this one simple and thorough enough for Small Businesses.

Four simple elements you can adjust, change, overhaul, or just leave as they are.

How do they define the products you are offering? What happens when we adjust them? Are they speaking with the same voice to the same targets and segments?

51

4.

"IF IT'S IMPORTANT ENOUGH TO DO, PROMOTE IT!"

This one frustrates me most about Small Businesses. They will spend weeks, months, even years! doing something for their business. Then they will launch it and barely making mention of it to existing customers or potential new customers. In that case, why bother doing it!

So if it's worth doing, it's worth promoting!

It isn't enough to put a few posts on social media, though by all means do that. But do more! Press releases, newsletters, emails, ads. Take ads! Invest in marketing! Tell the world. Tell them early and late and often.

5.

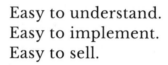

"FOLLOW THE "THREE EASYS" APPROACH."

Easy to understand.
Easy to implement.
Easy to sell.

Einstein believed that the whole world could be explained by very simple formulas. Easy needs to be a byword in every aspect of your business. But recognize, "easy" is not easy.

The easier you make it for your client to say Yes, the more likely they will. The easier it is to produce your product, the cheaper it will be. The easier it is for your team to understand a program, the better it will be implemented.

Constantly be asking yourself: How do I make it easier to....?

3.

"FIGURE OUT EXACTLY WHAT YOUR CLIENT WANTS—THEN GIVE THEM THAT."

This is the purpose of business. If you are not succeeding at this, you will not succeed.

Business fulfills needs. You need to understand which needs you are aiming to fulfill, then design each element of your business to fulfill those needs. Then communicate well that you fulfill these needs.

So analyze the needs of your customer base! Research them. Hell, even ask them! They'll tell you.

What do they want, how do they want it, how much do they want to pay for it? How do they want you to fulfill it?

54

6.

"CREATE UNITY-OF-MESSAGE THROUGH EACH ASPECT OF YOUR MARKETING."

I've mentioned the 4 Ps of Marketing. Product design, advertising and promotion, pricing and merchandising, positioning within the target. They need to not be in conflict, to speak with one voice, to pull the customer in one direction.

So often these elements are not in unison. Lower quality product with too high a price or vice versa. Even worse, messaging that belies the truth of the value being offered, shoddy look for great quality.

Understand where you want to be on the Price-Value scale and have that lead all aspects of your customer communication.

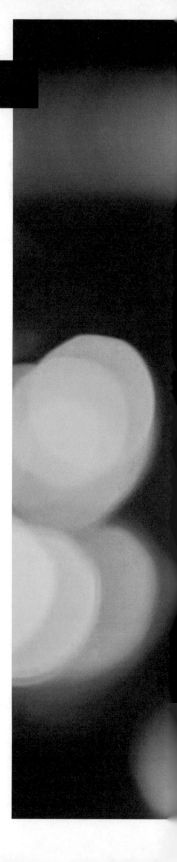

7.

"REWARD YOUR BEST CUSTOMERS IN MANY WAYS."

All your customers are not alike in terms of the Sales volume they can generate for your business. Classify your clients into three general categories: Large, Medium and Small and tailor your Sales programs based on where a client fits in one of the three categories.

Find ways to reward your best and potentially biggest clients because this is how you will survive in lean years and thrive in strong years. Discounts, better service, better deal terms, preferential choices, etc. These large-generating customers can be the difference in your long-term success.

8.

"SALES ARE BINARY: IT'S A ZERO UNTIL IT'S A ONE."

Business sales are binary: They are a Zero, that is, not a sale, until they are a One. There is no grey area here for Small Business. This is a mind-set Small Business entrepreneurs must have.

The change in status occurs when you have received cash or a deposit. Until that movement-of-money threshold has been reached, it's not a sale, it's not revenue, it's not anything of use, besides maybe interest.

Don't fool yourself that a promise, that an order form, or even a signed agreement is a One. Money transfers alone make a One, and until then....it's a zero.

9.

"MARKETING STRATEGY DEVELOPS THROUGH DEEP ANALYSIS."

To truly understand target segments, market reaction and competitive forces, one has to do substantial analysis. Here the importance of tracking outcomes, trying to find causes and effects, plays out.

Using tools such as Google Analytics, Facebook Ads manager and the like, along with your internal tracking tools in bookkeeping software, even you own questionnaires, are invaluable in producing insights into what your current and potential customers are reacting to and acting on.

These answers are in the analyses. Do them, do them regularly, and get a leg up.

10.

"START CREATING YOUR COMMUNITY & FOLLOWING YESTERDAY."

Don't wait to start building your community of friends, followers, supporters on social media. From Day 1 of the finalized idea, not from the launch into the market, but the existence of a final idea, start building your lists of names, emails, contacts, phone number. Start setting up your social media pages and start inviting your community to follow your pages.

There is no cost for this getting started early.
And it will be key on the day when you do want to launch to have as large a following as possible.

11.

"CREATE DETAILED CUSTOMER PROFILES."

To effectively create Marketing messages and supporting programs that work, we have to know *exactly, definitively* who we are talking to.

This is where Detailed Customer Profiles come in. Develop a profile of your Primary, Secondary and Tertiary targets.

Describe them in geographic, economic and other demographic terms. Know their ages, their income and education levels, where they live, where they can be found (advertising wise), what their interests are, etc. This analysis will drive better messaging and more effective ROI on advertising spend.

12.

"IF YOU'RE TARGETING EVERYONE, YOU'RE TARGETING NO ONE."

(And obviously you don't understand what the word 'target' means).

I can't tell you how many times a client has said to me their product or service is for everyone, everyone can use it, everyone will want it. Fact: There is almost nothing in this world that everyone likes, wants, needs, and they certainly like, want or need it equally.

Trying to create Marketing messages and programs that attract everyone is a ridiculous idea. So develop target markets to attack with your marketing, and even segments within those targets.

13.

"NAMES, COLORS, AND PHOTOGRAPHY MATTER MORE THAN YOU CAN IMAGINE."

Businesses are first defined in a customer's mind by their name, their logo and its colors, and the photographic imagery that is first communicated. As much as we marketers might wish it weren't so, first impressions are often lasting and linger in the mind even if they are changed later.

So spend the time, and more importantly, spend the money on professional graphic designers and on professional photographer from the start. They are a very worthy investment, perhaps your best investment at the inception of your business.

14.

"IN FIRST SALVOS, ALWAYS TALK ABOUT THEIR NEEDS."

The key to Sales is convincing the customer you can fulfill their need. But beginner marketers too often talk about secondary elements, cool features and unique properties without specifically addressing the customer's primary need. This is "Talking about what you want, not what they want."

In initial communication, always talk first and foremost about how you satisfy the needs of the client. Eventually there will be a time and place to mention more esoteric qualities. But if you don't achieve the first goal thoroughly, the second will never find fertile ground.

They came to you with needs, Tell them how you solve them.

63

15.

"YOUR MARKETING MIX NEEDS BOTH A CLASSIC & MODERN ELEMENT."

Too many businesses use only modern Social Media venues for their Marketing dollars when often, in many industries, classic "old school" marketing works well, sometimes even better.

In fact, studies show that a mix of old and new produces better results.

So of course, use social media, it's a great cheap option. But don't forget postcards, and other mailings. Or trade shows and industry publications. Even good old classic local and broader-venue advertising in print, radio, and even television.

16.

"IT ALWAYS COMES DOWN TO THE MESSAGE. SO TEST THEM."

Messaging IS that important to a business's success that the hours spent, thinking then analyzing then editing and re-editing your messages to your clients is well worth the time investment.

Because it is very possible to nail everything else, the price, product, placement, and then blow it all on bad messaging to your target market.

Here's where testing comes in. Test your messages. Try different ones to small groups of customers to ensure their effectiveness. Social media is great for this, especially Facebook, Tiktok & Instagram.

17.

"DON'T SEND YOUR SALES FORCE INTO BATTLE WITHOUT PROPER ARMAMENT."

Not meant literally, of course, but metaphorically, arm your sales force with professional websites, brochures, postcards, business cards, PowerPoint presentations, etc.

Whether you alone are the Sales force in a one-person form, or there is an actual team that you employ, recognize that the job is hard enough without great marketing materials to aid the process. In fact, it's nearly impossible without the tools.

Yes, these aids are a cash expense, but it is essential to think of them as an investment in the business!

18.

"DON'T WASTE COSTLY ADVERTISING SPACE TELLING PEOPLE WHAT THEY ALREADY KNOW."

It's Christmas!   It's Labor Day! It's Football Season! It's Hot!

We know!

People know this, they don't live under rocks. Advertising space, be it in a digital ad, on a store front window, in a radio or television commercial, on a billboard. Each of these is very limited in either time, space, or both in terms of a customer to see it and engage with it.

So to achieve your goal of communicating what want, despite these limitations, eliminate anything that people knows or understands already.

19.

"IN CHOOSING TARGET MARKETS, REMEMBER WHY JOHN DILLINGER ROBBED BANKS."

They asked famed bank robber John Dillinger why he robbed banks, and he famously responded, "Because that's where they keep the money!"

Too often Small Businesses focus their targeting on markets with the largest absolute size (ie., the most number of people) as opposed to targeting those with the greatest capacity to buy at a high margin. If the volume is good, but the average net amount is small, it will be a struggle. Often it's important to trade market size for purchasing capacity thereby going after where the money is.

20.

"SPEND MORE ON AD PLACEMENT THAN AD CONTENT."

I have run into this several times now with Small Business clients. Since they have not taken the time to plan their marketing correctly, doing comprehensive budgets beforehand, they spend too much on creating content leaving not enough to promote the content.

Don't get me wrong, creating good content is very important. But if no one sees the content because you don't have the cash left over to promote effectively, thoroughly, what good is it?

So do your budget, and plan more for ad buys and limit the ad creation spend. It'll lead to a bigger active community.

21.

"BE BOLD!"

You need to get noticed in an unimaginable avalanche of competitors as well as other messengers to your target audience. How do you cut through it?

Be bold! Be exciting! Be unique!

You don't have the budget to compete with larger companies. You can't match their capacity to reach out with diverse creative in various platforms.

But you can launch a campaign that people remember, that resonates with your audience and drives interest and activity. Avoid plain vanilla, avoid what's been seen a thousand times before.

22.

"BUILD DEAL / OFFER URGENCY."

As I've said rather brusquely in another tip herein, time kills deals. The longer they linger without completion, the more likely they never complete.

This is especially true in sales, and a great tool is the ability to limit availability and drive interest by shortening the opportunity window. This creates urgency in the target, forcing them to act timely or risk losing the opportunity.

True, don't make it too short. But let nothing linger by making all aware of the time limit and never launch any offer without an end date.

23.

"GET THE HOOK IN DEEP BEFORE YOU REEL IN."

Sales people, and people in general even in social situations, are so excited to make a sale, they go for the close through the ask before they've done enough work to secure the sale. Thus, I aim to get the hook in deep before pulling the reel.

To be sure, one can also wait too long to pull the trigger (sorry, graphic analogies), but going before making sure the client is ready as shown by their interest and eagerness has downfalls.

Prematurely asking for the close, before you've softened by sufficiently even thoroughly educating the client can negate the good work done before it.

24.

"DON'T DETAIL EVERY SINGLE ASPECT!"

Too often, Entrepreneurs oversell. They mention every little benefit and aspect of their business or their product so that it's too much for the potential customer to take in and actually turn off the lead.

It's important to remember that sales is not mentioning everything, it's finding the two to five essential things that a buying decision is predicated upon.

Study your sales to understand better the buying decisions, what motivated them, what were the closing factors. Then emphasize accordingly these aspects in your sales pitch and marketing materials.

25.

"TAILOR DIFFERENT MESSAGES TO DIFFERENT AUDIENCES."

While you should be consistent when communicating with a certain audience, no one ever said you have to say the same thing to every audience, in fact the opposite is true. Tailor your messages to different audiences based on each's audiences factors in their buying decisions.

Sometimes the differences in audiences is substantial (eg. individual vs corporate clients, regionalities, age) so we have to adjust our messaging and tailor what we're saying to the specific decision factors of each audience.

26.

"MEASURE FACTORS THAT AFFECT BUYING DECISIONS."

We need to always be looking for what is actually driving Buying decisions. Too often Small Businesses focus on an aspect in their marketing that's important to them, without understanding what's important to the customer. To help overcome this internal bias, I always recommend ranking aspects on a 1-5 scale of the importance of an aspect to the Buying decision.

Always ask: Will this element alter a buying decision? If so, by how much? Is it the difference between a sale and no sale?

Oftentimes price will be a important factor in the buying decision. Will the colors or attributes, the name, models in the ads, be an important factor?

75

27.

"IT'S OK TO FIRE BAD CLIENTS!"

Toxic is toxic and the sooner you eliminate the toxic from your business, the better. Even if it means taking a sales hit.

Bad clients come in many different shapes and forms. Some aren't respectful of what you bring to the table. Others don't pay on time or don't keep promises and guarantees they've repeatedly made.

For whatever the reason, too often too much time is spent trying to correct the situation with bad clients. This only steals away your most effective hours better spent on clients who do what they say and say what they're going to do. Focusing on these clients will create a better ROI and ROTI.

28.

"DO MORE MARKETING AT THE POINT OF SALE."

Briefly, sell at the point-of-sale. Your customer is there, at your store, at the moment of purchase be it digitally or physically. Sell them!

Make sure to deliver messages to the customer when and where they are making their purchasing decision. Studies show this is the most effective time to communicate with customers. Provide more information through signage (including pop-ups), perhaps discounts on additional or other complementary items etc.

They are a captive audience in or at your store which makes the opportunity so fertile.

29.

"DON'T GET TOO CUTE WITH YOUR MARKETING."

If it's over their head, it's under the line, and in the end the joke's on you. I've worked with some companies that were too smart for their own good with manifested marketing the target audience could not grasp. They forgot a golden rule of in sports: The best pass is the simplest pass.

Yes, many times, cool is valuable and esoteric is attracting. For those in on the joke, or inciteful enough to get the hip reference, it can be loyalty forming. It's true.

But don't shrink the market so much by limiting the in-the-know crowd too aggressively. We need more than six people and your mom to get onboard.

30.

"CONSIDER WELL PRICE ELASTICITY."

In economics and business, elasticity of price refers to the effect on sales of an increase in price of a product. If a price on a product is raised and there is a material drop-off in sales, the product is said to be price elastic. If there is no substantial drop-off in sales, it is said to be inelastic.

When raising the price of any product or service, one should always consider the elasticity be. Always ask the question thinking in terms of net absolute dollars: Will the increase I am passing through generate such a drop-off in sales that the net effect on absolute dollars is detrimental?

If there's a net detrimental absolute dollars, don't do the price increase.

31.

"HUSTLE IS THE BEST MARKETING TOOL."

Especially early on when your cash reserves are not plentiful: Networking, cold calling, presenting at events, etc. These are relatively low cost, but impactful tactics that can be very effective in both building a following and driving early sales.

While you must recognize that these efforts do not replace other marketing tactics, it can emphasize them and should work in coordination with them as in promoting events you're attending or presentations your making.

But hustle, the day-to-day pounding the pavement is essential tool for any start-up.

32.

"DEVELOP A VALUED LOYALTY PROGRAM."

From the most basic to the most complex, all forms of loyalty programs have generated both qualitative and quantitative results. It is not just the purview of giant corporations, Small Business can develop a host of different loyalty programs.

Perhaps a subscription program that gives added benefits to customers. Or maybe a running discount program which gives money back over time when certain threshold of sales are met. It can take countless shapes and sizes.

But these program lock customers into your business and incentivize them to not stray to your competitors and in fact increase their purchases over time.

81

33.

"CREATE THEN UTILIZE CONTENT ACROSS ALL MEDIUMS."

Since marketing dollars are often limited, look to create content that can work across multiple and even all different types of medium.

Create content that can work equally well in online ads, social media posts, YouTube videos and printed marketing pieces, email blasts, Tiktok etc. Recognize that single medium content is too expensive initially, and those that cannot be work across at least several mediums are not a good investment when cash levels are challenged.

In the future, when you are more cash solvent, you can specialize your marketing spend on medium specific content.

34.

"RECOGNIZE THE POWER OF INFLUENCER MARKETING."

We must accept the New World Order, meet the new boss and recognize Influencers.

Now obviously, Kim K. isn't doing a video for you. Nor is Mark Cuban to become a shareholder. But there are options for engaging smaller, more targeted influencers.

Look for those with local, loyal and very targeted followings. Many of them are dying to generate revenue from their following so that achieving a mutually beneficial exchange rate can be achieved.

35.

"USE YOUR GREAT REVIEWS TO THE MAX."

When I get a great verified legitimate review from a customer or client, I always have a slight desire to tattoo it on my ass and walk around buck naked.

Great reviews of your company or your service or your product, are Marketing Gold, and must be used as such through the telling of everyone early and often, like voting in Chicago elections (I kid). On your websites, in your emails, in your ads, in your conversations etc. etc. etc. Everywhere!

Because few things carry such weight with prospective buyers and clients such as a verified, legitimate review. Please note that I written verified and legitimate twice. Fake will be found out and a price will be paid.

36.

"ALWAYS SPEND ON SOCIAL MEDIA ADS"

I don't care if your business is being the local plumber or a new cooking utensil or a dating etc., everyone should be spending some money on social media ads. The ROI and risk return ratio of social media advertising such as Google, Facebook and Instagram is so extraordinary that every Small Business should spend something on social media ads.

In multiple cases, you can spend as little as one dollar a day in purchasing some ads. If you can't spend $300 a year in advertising to a targeted audience that social media provides, then you really need to revisit your business plan as something is wrong.

Find a dollar to spend here. Hell, find two or more.

37.

"EXPLOIT THE POWER IN TRADE INDUSTRY MAGAZINES."

Most industries, if they've been around long enough, have an Industry trade magazine or a webzine. I never know how they survive with such a limited targeted focus but they are there and they are a great resource for many things.

The most obvious one is advertising, but I want to emphasize strongly Public Relations promotion. Simply writing a press release and sending it into the magazine to get a blurb, or if you're lucky, a fuller article or profile can be the single most cost-effective promotional vehicle, especially if you write it yourself.

38.

"KNOW WHEN TO USE THE DIFFERENT SALES APPROACHES."

The two most common sales approaches are known as "Foot in the Door" approach and "Door in the Face" approach. The first approach asks for a small order in the hope of expanding in the future if, getting a foot in the door. The second approach asks for enormous order, often rejected, so that a smaller ask can be backed-up to and seems relatively minor.

The trick is to tailor your approach to the specific client and the specific situation. Pre-approach analysis of both of client and situation should govern which approach is used and will lead to strategic implementation.

39.

"DON'T FORGET ABOUT MERCHANDISING."

Merchandising is the sales process of presenting goods, originally in a physical store but also can apply now to online stores. Think of going into a furniture store and seeing an entire living room laid out or an online clothing store with full outfits on display. Even recommandations of matching pieces online. The presentation of a series of products together builds a greater value than seeing one product alone.

Further, merchandising also applies to developing offers for groupings of products. Think about deals on entire outfits or matching furniture pieces, like a sofa and table. Strategies that develop grouped purchasing are very effective in increasing average revenue per sales and store presentations should be designed with this in mind.

40.

"USE MORE & BETTER IN-STORE SIGNAGE"

There is no place better to talk to your customers then when they are there in your store thinking about making a purchase. It is the best time to not just inform them, but go further and market to them.

Don't just tell them the prices with a sticker on the product! Instead explain attributes, benefits and intangible qualities. Communicate the reason why they should Buy.

Sure, you can't just have books on shelves explaining every facet and detail (or can you?), but you can use additional, more thorough signage to achieve the goal of customer engagement, increased product knowledge and ultimately sale closing tactics.

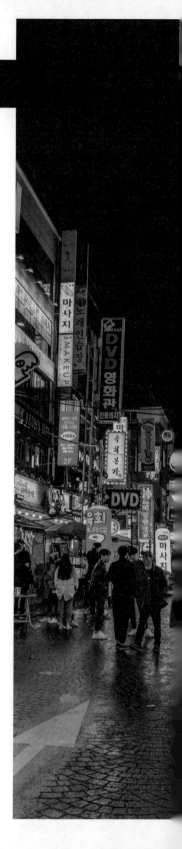

41.

"USE END-OF-SEASON SALES TO UNLOAD INVENTORY."

In many industries, inventory ages like fish. Meaning that past a certain season, the value of a product in the marketplace drops substantially once a season or two has passed. Think for example, the Fashion industry. Each quarter, certainly each year, the products you have in inventory are of less interest to your audience thus have less value. Here, stubbornness is not a virtue.

So it is essential to use end-of-season sales to unload aging inventory that is losing value. By moving product that is losing value, one can create free cash that can be used to buy new products

42.

"FIND WAYS TO DO SMALL SCALE MARKET RESEARCH."

A small business has to know what its customers are thinking. About the company's products, its marketing, even the company's values and ethics. This information is so incredibly valuable, one has to find ways to get this information from them.

The most surefire way is surveys and questionnaires, which are endlessly valuable when completed correctly. The company does not need to spend thousands of dollars to implement this, but basic interrogative efforts, asking two or three well-designed questions, can lead to important actionable knowledge.

43.

"REBRANDING HALFWAY IS IDIOTIC."

It's a little like leaving the house half-dressed, it leaves those who see you confused and wanting to run away.

Most businesses when they exist long enough, need to refresh and change substantially the visual projection of the company to the public, namely the logos, colors, even messages, etc. This is known as a rebrand or rebranding, and it can be a valuable tool to reset your placement with your target markets.

But make sure the rebrand is done completely. Wait and save until logos, websites, product packaging materials, store signage, everything can change, thereby work in unison with the same look and feel. A halfway completed rebrand builds confusion in the marketplace, as if two separate competing companies exist. And confusion is the last thing we want in business.

92

44.

"WRITE A FORMAL MARKETING PLAN WITH AN ITEMIZED BUDGET."

Business, when it is done right, is planned. It is not random, or by chance and luck. This is never more true than when it comes to marketing. The value of writing a formal Marketing plan with an itemized budget is almost incalculable.

Thoughtfully choosing, then detailing in writing the target markets, the methods and channels to speak to them, the messages, and very importantly along side is the budget per item. The amount of money you will spend on the various elements and channels in the marketing plan is paramount. It ensures proper allocation and implementation and protects against mission creep and overspending.

45.

"ALMOST ALL MARKETING PLANS HAVE TWO GOALS: EXPAND AND CAPTURE

While it's obviously true in new industries and product areas, it's still true in established domains. Almost all businesses have two Marketing goals: Expand the total Engageable market, and Capture more of the existing market. And your marketing should be split in some fasion between these two.

In general, if you increase the market size your business should capture its stable percentage. So a growing market, or a good economy, is more for you. But we must also always attempt to capture those already using the category from our competitors.

STRATEGY & PLANNING

Business strategy is generally defined as the planning and implementation of clearly-defined actions that are designed to achieve the goals and objectives of a business endeavor. This will normally include a discussion of the tactics that will be employed to bring about the desired ends.

While paralysis from analysis is a genuine problem for Small Business, it's converse, not enough strategic planning to make a sensible, implementable action plan that can be afforded and completed is the more prevalent problem. The time for strategic planning is hard to find when you are a one or two person organization. But find it you must. The time to think, strategize, formulate and reformulate must be essential tools in an entrepreneur's toolbox.

1.

"DON'T GET JUST ANY DEAL... GET THE RIGHT DEAL OR WALK AWAY!"

It is essential to know your worth, the worth of your product, the worth of the business, the worth of your deal to fare well in any negotiation. Insecurity, desperation breed diminished value and failure. Arm yourself with knowledge about your value through analysis.

Then have the courage to ask and hold out for your fair value. And don't let slick sales pitches sway you. And remember, the most important word in business is No.

2.

"ALWAYS, ALWAYS, ALWAYS KNOW YOUR COMPETITION!"

What are they doing strategically? Their prices, their messages, their promotions, their product mix and design. Business is often a zero-sum game, one's side's success is another side's downfall.

Time spent analyzing them will help you focus and refine your strategy in comparison to them. It may reaffirm your thoughts it may make you question your thoughts. Either way, it's analysis worth completing.

So go on, you have my permission, obsess over them, conspire against them to your benefit.

3.

"IN BUSINESS, IT IS BETTER TO BE LATE THAN WRONG."

"Life" happens in Business as it does in, well, life. How you respond to challenges is a key determinant of success in Small Business.

It's important to remember that you can recover from "Late" far easier than you can recover from "Wrong." Wrong has lasting implications and occasionally dire consequences that sometimes there is no recovery from.

So with decisions, with presentations, with deals and agreements, get it right even if you must delay. The potential consequences are demand delaying until all is right.

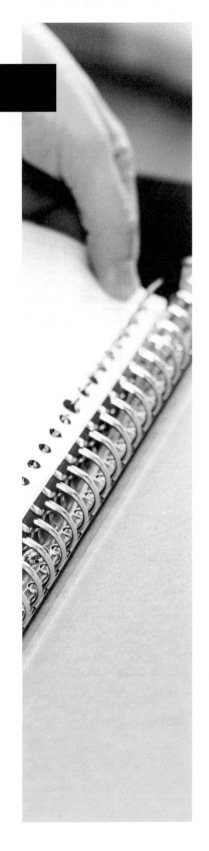

98

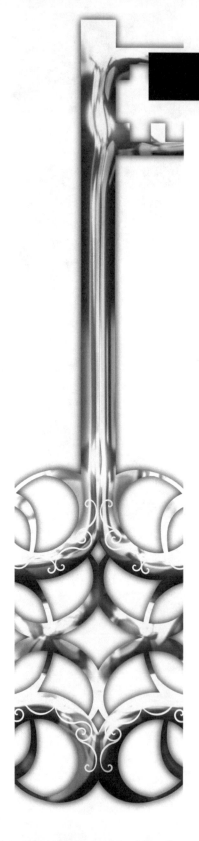

4.

"SPECIALIZATION IS THE KEY TO EARLY SUCCESS!"

Too many start-ups and Small Business try to do too much at their inception and in their first years. Too many products, too many services, too different business lines and even related businesses.

Too many of anything dilutes capital, be it time, marketing, or cash capital. Dilution in this case is a clear impediment to success.

Do one or two things great to start. After you've built a reputation and a community and refined your business model, expansion can happen. But only after!

5.

"A GUIDING PHILOSOPHY: UNDER PROMISE, OVER PERFORM."

Customer disappointment is a leading cause of lost revenue. And so often, one screw-up is the last screw-up you get a chance to make with a client.

The key to dealing with this is managing a client's expectations so you can always be a success or damn close to it. So push conservative estimates of production times, product abilities and success.

Remember please: Happy customers remain with you as customers, whereas unhappy ones are somebody else's revenue stream.

6.

"DON'T TRY TO BE ALL THINGS TO ALL PEOPLE AND MARKETS."

Even in the long-term, specialization is a key determinant of Small Business success. Many Small Business are intentionally and sometimes inadvertently pulled into different business lines and different product categories.

Business creep mitigates a lot of the good that has been established over the course of operations. Customers, suppliers need to understand clearly who your business is, what you bring to the table, and blurring these lines while chasing the new shiniest thing is a recipe for troubled results.

7.

"DON'T MAKE PEOPLE WORK TO DO...WHAT YOU WANT THEM TO DO."

This is one of my biggest pet peeves. We as businesses want our customers to do something. perhaps buy our product or see something on our website or call us or download something.

Make it easy for that to happen! Remove all hindrances. And obstacles. The easier it is for them to complete what we want, the greater number of them will actually complete it, whatever it is. So make it easy to email, to call, to buy, to recommend, etc.

So analyze yourself! And make things easy to find on the website. Make contacting you easy to do. Make ordering and paying simple as possible. And on and on and on.

8.

"EVERY COMPANY CONTENDS ON THE BATTLEFIELD OF LEGITIMACY AND CREDIBILITY."

It is the one thing of which *every company* in the world must convince its current and prospective customers. That your company is credible and legitimate in terms of your abilities to fulfill their needs.

And if you lose this credibility and legitimacy, it's often a fatal blow to a relationship, and sometimes even to a company. Because it's very hard to recover from a situation or event where you did not fulfill the expectations of the client.

So protect these elements as existential.

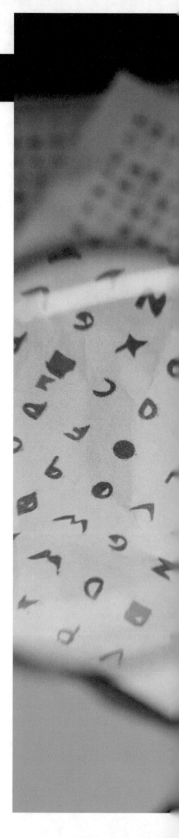

9.

"UNDERSTAND THE INTEGRATED PATH TO SUCCESS."

It is essential to understand how each element of a business must be worked together in unison with the other elements for better success. How finance makes marketing possible, and vice versa, and how strategy and management affect the other two together and must pull all in one direction.

10.

"IN A NEGOTIATION, FIRST DEFEND YOUR POSITION."

When receiving a counter offer, your first move...is not to move at all. Too many people, when receiving a counter offer to their proposal, immediately move to change their offer.

In fact, the right move is to not adjust your offer at all, but instead to defend it. Explain your position, explain why you choose it, defend its reasoning and soundness.

Moving is easy, and caving even easier. Defending your position first shows that you are not going be pushed around and that you believe in the efficaciousness of your proposal.

11.

"KNOW WHEN TO PULL THE TRIGGER ON CHANGE."

Flexibility is essential to Small Business success, and way too many Small Businesses wait way too long to make changes to their business model, their marketing, their financial structure. While it is important to give your plans enough time to take root and succeed in the marketplace, stubborn even slavish obstinance to something that isn't working is a death for an endeavor.

So early on, set-up guidepost and borderlines that will help you recognize when something has gone too long without success. Then do the necessary things for change (analysis, testing, implementation.)

12.

"START SLOW AND SMALL
WITH NEW CLIENTS."

Studies show that a customer/client is 7 times more likely to do something again than to do something for the first time. Studies also show that if a mistake is made on a first project or with a first purchase, the customer/client very rarely continues or repurchases with the supplier.

So I always suggest to Small Businesses to start slow or small with a new client to ensure that you can easily fulfill their needs thoroughly, expertly. Then after well achieving that, one has a better shot of renewing the relationship, enlarging that sale size or expanding your role with the customer.

13.

"SMALL BUSINESSES DON'T SPEND ENOUGH MARKETING DOLLARS TO SUCCEED."

If no one knows a business exists, does it make a sound when it goes bankrupt?

It may seem contradictory, but especially in the early years, Small Businesses need to spend more on Marketing, even when cash is hard to come by. Creating company and product awareness is indispensable. Too many businesses go out because they were not able to drive enough awareness because they didn't invest in marketing.

The good news: Marketing has never been this cheap or effective before thanks to Social.

14.

"CREATE, DEVELOP AND PROMOTE YOUR DIFFERENTIATING CHARACTERISTICS."

Why you, why your product or service? Why your company versus the competition? What are the reasons a client or customer should choose and yours over someone else. The answer is in your unique differentiating characteristics.

You need answers, and more importantly, you need to be thinking about your unique elements, creating them and developing them as you build your company. And then you need to prepare to be able to explain cogently to your target markets. Everyone needs a competitive response.

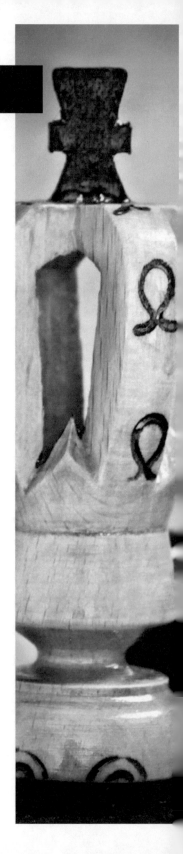

109

15.

"INVENTORY IS AN ALBATROSS THAT DROWNS NEW BUSINESSES."

Inventory sucks up your cash like a sponge, and for Small Businesses, it can be the source of a drowning death if it's not controlled and managed effectively.

Too many businesses want to launch and actually do with way too many different SKUs, too many products in too many variations. And they forget that inventory ages like old fish.

Start small! Fewer products in fewer variations. Let each SKU earn its place in your offering menu. This will free up cash for marketing while limiting downside if a poor product choice has been made.

16.

"CAN'T DRIVE FROM NY TO LA SANS MAP: PLANS ARE WRITTEN IN DETAIL & ORDER."

Planning is the mechanism by which strategy is organized for implementation. Yet too many Small Businesses, if they do planning at all, don't formalize planning into a useful written form. So too often they run ahead on projects without planning, and then find themselves lost somewhere on the route.

Write down the idea fully, then detail the steps needed to implement it in the order they need to occur. This act actually forces you to clarify thoughts and brings your focus to the small steps that lead to successfully launches.

17.

"DON'T GET EVERY LAST DOLLAR IN A NEGOTIATION."

You may think it wise, admirable or desirable to extract every last bit you can from the opposite negotiating party, but in effect it's short-sighted, and often short circuits future benefits and stability.

Oftentimes, you will need to work with the opposite party to fulfill on whatever was being negotiated. Other times, tough negotiations leave a bad humor over a deal, with the opposite side looking for any excuse or option to cause unpleasant aftereffects.

A deal works best when it works well enough for both sides.

18.

"EARLY ON, DO MORE OF WHAT YOU DO WELL AND TRY LESS NEW THINGS."

Especially in Small and newly started businesses, the cult of the New is too dominant in mindsets. Growth will come more through expanding what you already do than from trying to expand into new things, be it new product categories, new business lines, new industries.

While eventually, when a solid basis of cash flow and positioning in the marketplace have been established, expansion can occur, focus efforts (time, money) on expanding existing business lines and growing average customer spend. ROI is here.

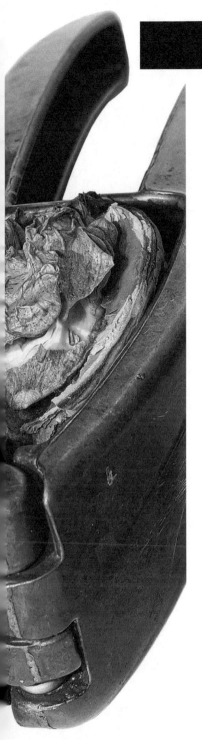

19.

"LEARN TO USE LEVERAGE GENTLY."

In Business, there are times when you have to use the leverage a situation has given to achieve a necessary end. Perhaps with suppliers who need your cash or clients who need you to deliver on time with quality work.

But too often, new businesspeople use their leverage very heavy-handedly, without understanding the long-term perspective of this. Business is circular, and leverage swings, and people remember how you used your leverage against them, whether gently or with a brick to the head.

Remember the wheel turns.

114

20.

"CREATE COMPANIES, NOT PRODUCTS."

Too many early entrepreneurs focus solely on a single product, one that they want to bring to market, without considering that very rarely is a company successful with just one product.

It is important to understand the mindset of a potential investor or lender, and think through what they are looking for in a potential investment. In a word: Diversification.

A company with expansion opportunities and diversified revenue streams are far more likely to garner interest than the sole product company without with limited expansion opportunities.

21.

"DO EXPANSION PLANNING BEFORE YOUR START THE BUSINESS."

Don't be afraid to think of what might be. Hell, this is often the most fun part. And expansion planning needs to happen before you start the business and be something you return at least annually as it acts as road to where you are going.

I always think of the scene in the film Apollo 13, where Tom Hanks needs to keep the moon in the window to course correct. New product expansion, new market expansion, or even funding expansion to make your other plans happen. Planning is making sure your moon is in the window, and you are heading towards it. Do it early and often.

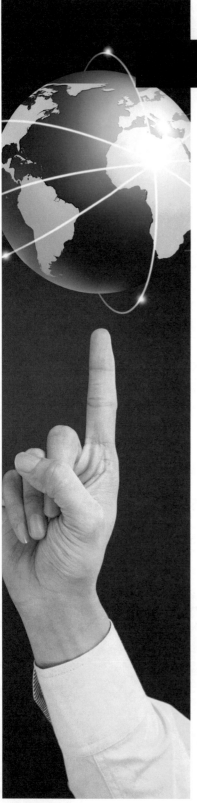

22.

"LEARN TO USE LEVERAGE GENTLY."

In Business, there are two categories of expansion: Horizontal and Vertical.

Horizontal expansion is usually defined as adding new additional products related to existing product offerings.

Vertical expansion is defined as adding geographic markets to the original launch market.

When planning your growth, you want to focusing on both types of expansion. Each version diversifies your revenue sources and augments the company's capacity to generate cash and survive enviable economic downturns.

117

23.

"WE ALWAYS ASK."

We do it politely, respectfully, confidently, but we always ask. We always ask for the discount, for the price increase, for the more, the less, the inclusion or deletion or whatever is the case We always work up the courage, steel ourselves and ask for what we want or need.

No one is going to just give you ever benefit and essential element. Maybe they don't think about it, maybe they don't want to. It's on you to ask. Asking is a skill every entrepreneur needs to develop.

As I've said elsewhere, be prepared to defend your position behind your ask and understand that the answer may be some form of No.

118

24.

"CREATE SUBSTANTIALITY."

An essential thing for Small Business, especially those with only one or a few team members, is to create a sense of substantiality in your business. You want to seem bigger than you are because many companies if not most want to work with bigger more established enterprises because there is risk in working with Small companies.

So how do we do it? Make sure marketing materials are first class: websites, brochures, business cards, video presentations. Make sure customer-facing interactions happen on a top-level: meetings, client meals, contracts. It's about seeming larger, more established than you may be.

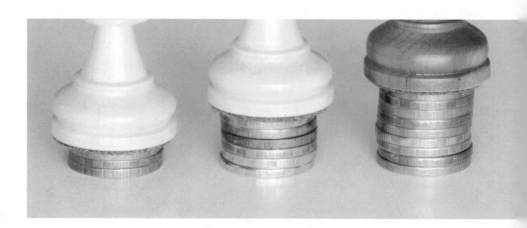

25.

"DECIDE WHICH CONTRACT POINTS TO DIE ON."

As I've said elsewhere, business is done in writing which means letter agreements, engagement letters and formal contracts (all largely the same purpose) are completed between parties in a business relationship. In my business, I don't work without one.

In each agreement, there are things that are good to have and things you need to have. You need to know which is which BEFORE you begin discussions as it should govern how you negotiate. Where you defend, where you acquiesce, where you walk away should be thought through, known and managed accordingly.

26.

"MAKE INVESTMENTS IN YOURSELF AND THE BUSINESS."

Too many Business owners don't and even refuse to make investments in their business and themselves when times are good, and the business is generating sufficient cash flow.

Like Gollum cherishing his ring to the detriment of his life, owners keep their cash and stroke it. But the key is to invest it in the business, wisely, prudently, but substantially.

Perhaps it's new computers and systems, perhaps its bigger investments in marketing, or even just advanced educational programs for key employees or the CEO. But we are looking for investments that will pay future returns to the business.

27.

"DON'T LET SOMEONE OR SOME BUSINESS HAVE TOO MUCH LEVERAGE OVER YOUR BUSINESS."

In the stock market they say that diversification is the only free lunch. It's true in business as well. The greater any one element has control over key aspects of your business, the more risky your business is because of the outsized leverage that element can impose on you.

Be it clients, employees, suppliers or financiers, it's essential to develop diversification of sources into your business. Too much leverage in the hands of one outside force must be mitigated through finding other comparable sources.

The benefit will show itself in the inevitable negotiations that will occur between equal parties.

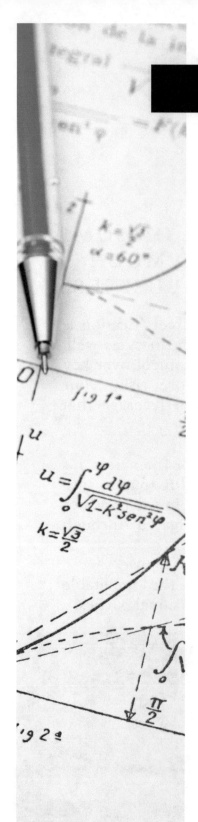

28.

"RIDE THE BUSINESS MATURITY CURVE."

Most Small Businesses start as fledging enterprises, a one or two person shop with often little resources, experience and knowledge. And that's OK to start. But only at the start.

Small Business must ride the Maturity curve. As they grow, as they expand, they must begin to add those classic Business elements that were not there at the start.

Add relevant Accounting and Control systems, add automated platforms for Marketing, add insurance and retirement plans for all parties.

Add those elements that will bring a return in many facets mostly ensuring more sustainable future growth.

29.

"DON'T TRY TO SWALLOW A WHALE IN ONE BITE."

It's the business version of your eyes are bigger than your stomach. Giant order are great, giant orders are what Business dreams are made of. But only when your business is prepared to fulfill perfectly.

What happens is the Business owner doesn't fully comprehend the effect a giant order can have on the business. Many different areas will be effected including cashflow, customer service, production, inventory systems and other client relations.

The Smart Move? If you're unsure you can fulfill, ask to cut the order to a more manageable size. In the long run, you'll be respected and rewarded.

30.

"GETTING CARRIED WITHIN A BIG STORE OR CHAIN, ISNT THE END BUT THE BEGINNING OF WORK."

Imagine you've just got approved to have a product carried by a giant retailer, either online or brick and mortar. Think Amazon or Home Depot. You're there in the store! And so what?!

It is then that the real work of marketing and selling must begin. The average Home Depot store has 200,000 SKUs and you're just one among them. Forget about Amazon.

Yes you've done great work to get yourself carried b the large retailer. Now is the time to invest in Marketing and promotion to capitalize on it. Because if you're in the stores and no one knows it, nothing happens, certainly not sales.

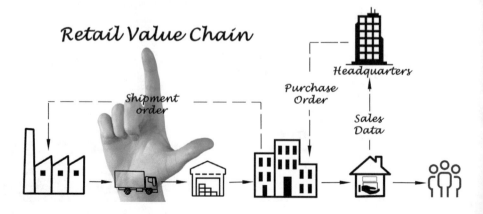

Retail Value Chain

Shipment order

Purchase Order

Headquarters

Sales Data

31.

"GET TO THE DECISION-MAKER."

When you're a Small Business trying to make large sales to substantial companies, there are usually several levels of "Management" that need to be waded through to close the deal. Your goal is to get to the decisionmaker as soon as possible to minimize wasted time.

This is the person whose Yes or No ends in a sale...or ends the sale. Ask questions *subtly* to find out who that is, then work to include them in sales discussions, presentations, proposals, negotiations etc.

But remember: Each level can kill your sale so it is important to pay the appropriate respect, as time-consuming and soul-sucking as it may be,

32.

"MAKE YOURSELF INDISPENSIBLE."

This is essential for an provider, be it consultant or Scranton paper supplier. Your goal is to become indispensable to your client. That means there survival depends on your product.

When you have insinuated yourself or your product in a client / customer's life or business, many leverage doors open up to you including the ability to raise prices or negotiate better deal terms. Of course there are levels of indispensability, and perfect indispensiblity does not exist.

Do your job perfectly and expand it in the operations. Design your product perfectly so that it uniquely fulfills a need. Many routes, one goal: Indispensable.

127

33.

"BE, AND WORK WITH, DEAL-MAKERS."

Over time in business, you will find often that people tend to fall into two different groups: Deal Maker or Deal Breaker. Sometimes it's the job of certain people to be deal-breakers like lawyers, financial consultants, accountants. They're trying to protect the company, and so their jobs and natures lead to obstacle-building and hesitancy

But deal-makers are always looking for a way to close deals and find solutions when obstacles. They know that no perfect deal exists, they know they will not get everything they want, and they remain confident they can make the deal work out in the end irrespective of the final terms ultimately negotiated. We want to be deal makers.

34.

"LEARN HOW TO TRAIN YOUR CLIENTS."

It's a tough but necessary skill because we have this ingrained idea that the customer is always right. But overtime it is important to train your client to work with you and accept your products and services in an appropriate and mutually beneficial manner.

We cannot allow customers to not respect us or act to our businesses detriment. If we allow it, it will only continue so it is essential to act.

This takes training your clients which needs to be done over time. It takes subtly correcting and redirecting inappropriate attitudes and behaviors towards more respectful and fruitful actions and modes of communicating.

129

35.

"RUN TO REVENUE."

This is a call to not be distracted when a real revenue opportunity is close at hand. Distractions can come in myriad forms, other clients, other problems, even other revenue opportunities. I am making the case for concentration on one opportunity at a time, recognizing other things can wait their turn.

This is special important for Small Businesses where certain sales or deals can be life or death, certainly game-changing. But often owners lack the single focus, get distracted, and let their attention drift to other things.

There is a time for everything, and everything in its turn. When revenue is at hand, run towards it. Run as fast as you can at it undistractedly.

36.

"PLANT YOUR FLAG FIRST WHEN NEGOTIATING."

This one has two schools of thought, launch first or wait, and I believer in going first in negotiations. Stating your offer first as opposed to responding to someone else's first salvo is beneficial.

Planting your flag first with the terms and conditions that you want saves time and shapes the negotiations in your favor. It gives you an opportunity to explain and defend your position before anything else is discussed, communicating the needs and wants (know the difference between those two) necessary to reach an agreement. In the event of an insurmountable difference between the parties, time is saved. If it's manageable, everything has been laid out in the beginning.

37.

"DEVELOP KPIS THAT ARE ESSENTIAL TO MEASURE PROGRESS."

KPIs, the acronym for Key Performance Indicators, are statistics about the business that are measured and tracked over time, and that indicate if the business is making progress on various fronts deemed important.

Examples often used are the number of Social Media followers, the amount of visitors to websites in a given month, the number of purchases made on a website in a quarter, etc. One can set-up almost endless different KPIs and it's important to tailor to your specific business and industry.

But Remember: Sales, Gross Margin, Cash Flow and Profitability are the ultimate KPIs.

38.

"ASK FOR AN NDA / CONFIDENTIALITY AGREEMENT."

NDA stands for Non-Disclosure Agreement, and along with Confidentiality Agreements which are similar and often serve the same purpose, aim to protect the ideas behind a company and its product offerings.

All businesses should ask an outside party they're going to work with to sign a document or include language in their agreement that protects private or confidential information

Please note that I wrote Ask, not Insist. Larger, well-established companies will often not sign these because they are involved in so many projects and businesses. Given their reach, they cannot reasonable sign one.

39.

"USE EMAIL TO DELAY, DEFLECT, AND NEGOTIATE."

Sometimes in business, the other side has more power, more influence or just more sheet brute force as a function of age, experience and even size. Everyone gets intimidated sometimes, and dealing with folks who have some advantage puts us by definition at a disadvantage.

Caving in is not the answer. However, buying yourself time to gather your strength and courage is a tactical lifesaver, and I've found email to be a great tool for it. Email allows us to think through our answers, word them more carefully and write things we could not otherwise say face-to-face.

Long-term, avoidance doesn't work. But using email to choose the time, placc and fashion of a response often produced better results.

40.

"GET SOMETHING WHEN YOU GIVE SOMETHING."

Negotiating is a learned skill. While some people are born negotiators personality wise, no one's perfect at the start A great rule to follow is to understand that giving something is an opportunity to get something from the other party in return.

The key is analyzing their Ask, and making an assessment of its value then developing your Ask in response. Then finally having the courage, the steel in the spine to declare your Ask in return.

But never let an opportunity to enhance your situation slip away when fulfilling a needed request from a counterparty. When take when we give in business.

41.

"PARTICIPATE IN / LEAD YOUR CLIENT'S STRATEGIC PLANNING."

With the goal of becoming indispensable to your clients, ask to participate in their business's strategic planning sessions, and sugges and even offer to lead them if client doesn't plan or do strategy planning sessions.

Often times it is the supplier of either a service or product that has a better view of how an end-user can grow its business. In these cases, it's the product or service supplier who needs to be developing strategic reviews of their client's growth trajectories.

Because in the end, the growth of the client is the growth of the supplier, and the girls that comes from a great idea is a win-win all around.

MANAGEMENT & EXECUTION

This section concerns the actual running of the business, which in its way, makes all the other sections possible. For if we cannot manage the business (receive payments, pay bills on time, hire staff, manage bank accounts, etc.), one really needs to shut down and look for a more stable and achievable employment opportunity.

But beyond the base necessities above, real business management is about execution of the strategic plan. Execution is often the difference between unattainable ideas and real corporate success. It is the hard work behind the fun parts of strategy building and ideation.

While often not glamorous, it is the undergirding of business success, for what good is a plan if you cannot implement well enough to achieve what is wanted.

1.

"EVERYONE HAS VISIONS. VISIONARIES MAKE THEIRS COME TO LIFE SUCCESSFULLY."

While I won't say that Great Ideas are a dime a dozen, so many great ideas don't succeed, let alone ever launch, because what it takes to implement a great idea is completely different from what it takes to dream up an idea. Real business genius is in the former.

So focus on the ability to pull together a grand array of skills in achieving initiatives. Execution of decisions, the usage of personal agility and management timing is how real visionaries create shareholder wealth.

2.

"NEVER FORGET ABOUT "ROTI!"

Return On **Time** Investment (ROTI).

Everyone remembers to focus on ROI, Return on Investment, and rightly so. But far too many forget about ROTI and for Small Businesses, it is equally essential.

Time is as limited and as limiting as cash. We must all make decisions constantly about whether this project, this client, this investment is not only worth it on a financial perspective but also on a time perspective.

There is a Time Opportunity cost of pursuing things that are not worth the effort.

139

3.

"THE DIFFERENCE OF SUCCESS & FAILURE IS OFTEN KNOWLEDGE AND EXPERIENCE."

The idea that you will start your business as a first-time entrepreneur with all the necessary skill sets for success is absurd. This is not a comment on your specific talents, it's just that no one arrives freshly into the business world fully formed.

And knowledge and experience matter to success in business!
So find the talents and experience in others that you don't have. Hire those with skills you don't possess, bring in consultants to round out your skill sets.

It can't be about pride, not now, you have too much risking on it. If you don't have the knowledge or the experience, get someone who does and learn from them.

140

4.

"FIND GOOD PEOPLE, GET GOOD PEOPLE, KEEP GOOD PEOPLE!"

That is, pay them enough so they stay in both money AND respect!

Your business, whatever it is, is people. Someone great, at whatever it is (sales, accounting, customer service, purchasing) is so essential to the long-term success of a business. But too often, companies lose their great people because they don't fully understand how important these people are.

Find a way to keep them if you think they are truly great. Reward them, inspire them.

5.

"IN THE MODERN ERA, DISTANCE IS NOT A LIMITATION."

The world has changed, change with it. Tools such as Zoom, Skype, Free Conferences, WhatsApp, etc. have expanded Business horizons and now great services need not be in the same room.

From Cost savings to skills upgrading to expanding your representation, Virtual Consultants are the best route to success Schedule meetings, calls and work when it's convenient for you, not when your consultant has enough time to come to your office.

Get the Best help for you, not the closest. The world has so much to offer.

6.

"MAINTAIN LOWER HIGHS AND HIGHER LOWS."

Creating a business, any type of business is tough, very tough. And it will have so many ups and downs along the way to success that it is important to develop a strategy for managing the emotions, the ebbs and flows of happiness and fear.

I speak often to clients of maintaining Lower Highs and Higher Lows in managing emotions. Extremes are where problems arise, and extremes are rare.

So don't get too excited when something great happening, and keep it measured similarly, when something bad happens. Few things are truly fatal.

143

7.

"THE MOST IMPORTANT WORD IN BUSINESS IS... NO."

It's easy to say Yes. It's fun to say Yes. But things that are fun and easy are often not what's best for your business. As a result, one of the essential skills to develop as one becomes an entrepreneur and CEO of their own company is the ability to say No.

You will disappoint some people with this for sure. Perhaps employees who want a raise or suppliers who want bigger orders or investors who want to buy shares at a low price. Then is the time to gather courage and backbone and say No.

8.

"BUSINESSES WITH PARTNERS ARE LIKE MARRIAGES WITH MORE DIVORCE."

As a result of the above, one can't overestimate the importance of the decision of who you partner with because at some point, problems will arise.

I'm not saying that many partnerships won't work, last or become successful, but it's important to recognize that enterprises, and the people who own them, change over time. Their visions for what the company is, should or could be, can change, diverge, and divide.

So choose wisely. Divorce sucks everywhere, and especially so in business when friends and maybe family are involved.

9.

"GREAT EXECUTIVES LEARN TO USE ALL THEIR VOICES."

Effective management is focused on getting things done. In the course of that, a great executive will use a broad range of people-affecting voice tones including knowing when to joke, when to flirt, when to pressure, when to raise their voice in anger.

It's important to develop the ability to well tailor your responses to what a situation demands, be it conflict and problem or new relation and sales opportunity.

The best executives work to develop these skills in less urgent situations so the talents are there in the big moments.

10.

"DON'T HESITATE TO BRING IN PAID CONSULTANTS."

Socrates tells us that knowledge of ignorance....is wisdom. Most entrepreneurs know their industry well. Certainly, this is the most essential. But that doesn't make them experienced business people.

Especially in the beginning of a venture, you increase your chances of success tremendously by hiring consultants with skills you do not possess.

This may seem a little self-serving, but that doesn't make untrue. Penny-wise & pound foolish is not a path to success, it's an ego trip. Spend for the best.

11.

"THERE'S ALWAYS A CHEAPER WAY TO DO THINGS."

This contradicts somewhat with the previous, but these days we can leverage technology to do some many things cheaper than ever before. And it's more than all right to use them, as we cannot let perfection be the enemy of the very good.

One can have an excellent website without coder. One can use Google's free Office suite instead of Microsoft's. One can accept credit cards cheaply. Even this book can be written with Canva's free service instead of graphic designer.

In almost every field cheaper, cash saving options exist. Find them, use them.

12.

"CONSTANTLY BE EDUCATING YOURSELF."

One of your main jobs is to get better at business. It is the job of all of us over the course of our career. And studies show that executives that are learning and improving end up making more money in the end.

So read and research and study and invest in learning in general. With so many changes happening in each facet of business, if you are not staying up-to-date, if you are not investing time and money in the self-growth processes that improves you as a Business-person, you and your business will be left behind and at a competitive disadvantage.

13.

"THE SECOND MOST IMPORTANT WORD IN BUSINESS IS...SLOWDOWN."

Errors happen with speed in business. When people rush to make decisions without the proper analysis and effective forethought, all manner of hell can break loose.

So slow down. Slow. Down. Few things are truly so urgent and emergent that a decision needs to be made now, a conversation needs to be had now, a purchase needs to be completed now.

Now!....is the enemy of effective management.

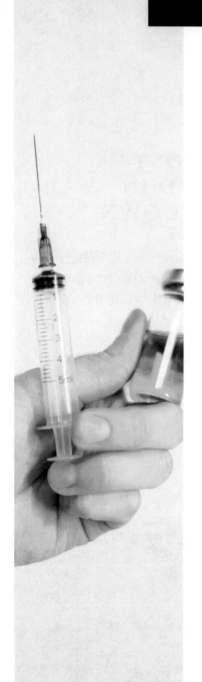

14.

"A HEALTHY DOSE OF SCEPTICISM, DOUBT AND SUSPICION IS ESSENTIAL."

More than essential, this is obligatory. Entrepreneurs by their very nature are almost always optimistic people and sometimes to a fault. But never forget that the business world is full of shady people, or even just people not completely above board trying desperately to survive in their endeavors.

Given this world, it is just plain necessary to have doubt and a skeptical view of promises, guarantees, and other claims being made to you.

"Trust but verify" comes later. "Doubt and tread very careful" comes first.

15.

"STOP BULLSHITTING YOURSELF."

This is the most common problem I find with Small Business entrepreneurs. They begin to believe their own bullshit. In terms of their title or their role, what they've achieved or what they plan to do, too many begin to believe their story pitch they're giving others, though knowing deep down it's rife with stretching and exaggeration to use kind words.

So keep reality and truth close at hand always. Remember, while you may be CEO of your "start-up," you're also the person who makes copies, and you haven't created Apple yet, Mr. Jobs.

Truth is the valuable currency.

16.

"A GOOD ACCOUNTANT, LAWYER & BUSINESS CONSULTANT ARE WORTH THEIR WEIGHTS IN GOLD."

It really is "Not What You Get, But What You Keep." And these specialists are what help you keep more. Recognize that it is impossible for you to know all the things you need to know to be successful. There's no shame in this, it's true of every business person.

The error is in not bringing in outside help. Go get help from people who know what you don't! Because oftentimes the difference between success and failure is knowledge and experience.

17.

"IN START-UPS, 1/3 OF CEO TIME NEEDS TO BE FOCUSSED ON RAISING CAPITAL."

At least one third in fact! Maybe 50%, depending on the severity of the need.

There is no one else in the organization that can do deals on a capital raise other than the CEO. It's who investors want to deal with and it is the only person with the knowledge and power within an organization to bring to bear what is necessary to succeed in a capital raise.

So arrange your daily / weekly efforts accordingly and commit to this time investment. Work with brokers if need be, pull in your CFO as needed, but this essential element can't be outsourced but too many try to.

154

18.

"PLEASE & THANK YOU: ONE SHOULD NOT UNDERESTIMATE COURTESY & POLITE."

As so much of successful business management is the skillful handling of relationships, *courtesy, respect and politeness* go much further than many most realize.

Whether you are dealing with customers and clients or suppliers or service providers, but most importantly with your employees, show your respect for the help they give you and the job they do for you. Do this with the minimum modicum of outward manifestation of it, the simple embodiment of courtesy and respect by *always* using Please and Thank you.

19.

"SO MUCH OF BUSINESS SUCCESS IS TIED TO THE SKILL OF MANAGING RELATIONSHIPS."

If I could give every entrepreneur one skill more than any other, it would be the capacity to manage relationships well. To be able build trusting and mutually beneficial connections with the entire range of interactions: employees, suppliers, bank managers, consultants, and of course, customers.

I cannot stress enough the importance of concentrating on and developing this skill as one goes through their journey of becoming an entrepreneur business owner. Like all things, one needs to work at it to become better.

20.

"REAL BUSINESS IS DONE IN WRITING."

It surprises me how often I need to remind businesses that business is written, it's agreed-to and memorialized in writing.

Be it contracts and engagement letters, or invoices and email confirmations, write down to communicate what has been agreed or occured by the two parties. Ephemeral, be damned.

It's not insulting, to the contrary, it's professional and it's smart. Because different interpretations and disagreements will arise, and it's better to have a written verification of what was decided and/or even discussed.

Warning: Beware those who don't or won't put things in writing.

21.

"MAKE EVERYTHING SHORTER."

From your emails to your marketing messages to your meeting lengths, be they on video or in-person, make everything in your business and the running of it *shorter*.

Studies show the limits of people's attention spans and their capacities to be productive in a consecutive period of time is far shorter than we believe. So the old adage in writing is true everywhere: Less is more.

So if you want to be more productive meetings, marketing and staff, shorten all interactions regardless of the medium the interaction is occurring in.

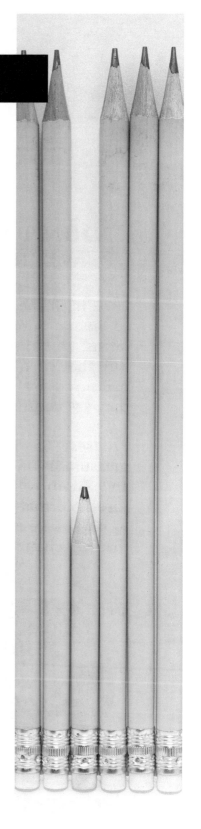

22.

"DON'T CONFUSE ACTIVITY WITH REAL PROGRESS."

I see it all the time, people running around doing so many things and dropping all the new sexy terms, thinking they are advancing their causes. But they're not, they're not making headway as measured by sales, margin and profits, because they are confusing *activity with progress.*

Progress is measurable in the numbers, it's measurable in cash. So stop the endless meeting and Zoom calls that lead nowhere. Have a higher threshold that activities must pass in order for you to undertake them. And certainly focus on things that will change the metrics of business success.

23.

"DON'T WORK WITH ASSHOLES."

Maya Angelou once said, "When someone shows you who they are, believe them the first time."

Life is too short, and success is so dependent on people that it's really advisable to not work with assholes. They come in all shapes and sizes, and I promise you this, eventually, in the end, it will be not be worth it.

Sometimes you don't know they're assholes at first, and sometimes you can't extricate yourself from the relationship immediately. But once it's clear, and often it's clear right away, get moving out, get moving away, then move on completely when you can.

24.

"BE FINISHERS OF THINGS."

When we are Small Business owners, our job is to finish things, not just move the ball forward. We finish, then move on to the next and then we finish that. It's the completion that counts.

Too often, I see so many entrepreneurs get 10 projects half-way home without remembering that if you always move 50% closer, you never get to your destination.

So finish things to their ultimate conclusion than launch them into their appropriate realm. There is nothing wrong with revisiting later, as long as the first salvo when completed and launched.

25.

"PICK ADVISERS WHO ARE NOT YOUR FRIENDS."

In the conversations with my father before he would ground me, he would always say, I'd love to be your best friend, but I *have to be* your father." The corollary applies to between entrepreneurs and their advisers. Don't take friends as advisers.

First, friends care about you and don't want to see you hurt, disappointed, questioning yourself etc. They will tend to agree and support. But advisers have to do the dirty work, the unpopular job of telling you your mistakes, errors, and poor decisions. You want them to. You need the truth unvarnished yet hopefully tactfully delivered.

26.

"LEARN TO ASK FOR HELP, EARLY AND OFTEN."

Too many new business people get stuck on the point of pride of trying doing it all themselves. Whereas smart entrepreneurs know the need to build a network of talented resourceful, and most of all, generous people to give you help, advice, consideration etc.

Learning to ask for help is one of the most important skills every entrepreneur needs. No one makes it alone, everyone makes it through the kindness, patience and contributions of outside resources

One thing though: When you make it big yourself....pay it back later for the next young entrepreneur.

27.

"GET USED TO USING THIS PHRASE: LET ME THINK ABOUT IT."

Often in important meetings be they key sales, investor or even employee meetings, something will come up that you are not prepared for. In these instances, a good stall is better than a bad decision.

Too many new entrepreneurs feel forced to respond immediately as if reflecting will make others question their competency or authority. Wise, senior executives learn to deflect in order to reflect.

Never feel pressured to respond to "bearhugs", which is what being forced to respond is called in business. The world won't end with a delayed response. And people who bearhug are not who you want around.

28.

"ALWAYS WALK THE TALK."

It's highlighted there in the photo below: Integrity. Doing what you said you would do. Walking all the talk you speak.

Each relationship in a business, from management to employee, from provider to customer, from banker to lendee, and on forever depend on integrity, the following-through, the keeping of your words and promises.

It is impossible to overestimate the value of integrity on business relationships. It can easily be the make-or-break element between for success, and its absence lead to failure over time. And rightly so.

29.

"TAKE CARE OF THE PEOPLE WHO TAKE CARE OF YOU."

It should be understood without saying, and usually is with high producing team members, but I am arguing here for taking care of all team members who are taking care of you well.

From high to low, we must reward those doing great jobs and who go the extra step for us thereby allowing us to be successful, from the office cleaners to the computer techs, the secretaries who really run our lives.

Take care of the poeple who are taking care of you. Oftentimes, it's money, but not always. Sometimes it's extra vacation so they can recharge. Othertimes, it's health insurance, or retirement accounts and stock ownership. It all adds up.

30.

"FIGURE OUT IF YOU ARE AN ARTIST OR BUSINESS PERSON"

Good business people rarely make good artists, and good artists very rarely make good business people. I wish it were otherwise, but it's not.

The Greek Oracle instructed us to Know Thyself, and it's ever true in business too. Are you an artist or are you a business person? You need to know and admit the truth to yourself.

It is OK to not have the right temperament. It is NOT OK not to recognize it and take appropriate steps to overcome it. Bring on Business people to offset your deficiency. Fear not. Often the combination of artist and business produces even greater results.

31.

"EVERYTHING IS YOUR JOB."

You need to accept this, and instill it in your bones and your mode of being.

Too often, new managers are looking to only do to the fun things, the things they like, the things that have a tangible outcomes. But as the CEO of the company, everything is your job, everything is your responsibility. And if things don't get done right and don't get finished on time, it's on you.

Yes, you need to delegate and outsource. That is essential to growth. But it does not obviate the need for the Boss to keep their fingers on the pulse and step in to finish any and everything when necessary.

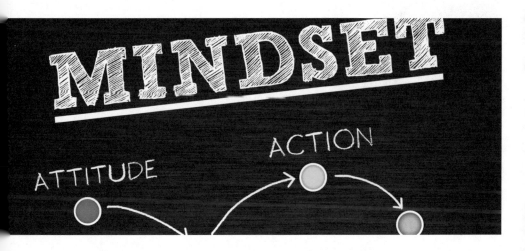

32.

"RECOGNIZE WHAT YOU CAN DO AND WHAT YOU CAN'T."

Socrates tell us that Knowledge of ignorance is wisdom. There is a corollary in abilities, and self-knowledge is essential for success. Each of us has talents in some areas and weakness in others. Our job in business is to figure these things out quickly, then make appropriate decisions based on the answers.

That is, fill your holes with others that have the skills you do not. If you're anti-conflict, get someone to handle the businesses conflicts. If you're not the Sales type, hire salespeople who can do what you cannot.

Recognizing honestly and early your deficiencies, then finding complimentary skills in others will lead to success.

169

33.

"THERE'S NO SENSE SETTING RULES IF YOU DON'T LIVE BY THEM."

Yes, you're the owner, you're the boss. But your employees, consultants, clients, everyone, notice hypocrisy what faced with it. To install compliance with rules set up to help the company, the owner has to follow them too.

But again and again, I see the Small Business people set up rules like limitations on T&E or sales discounts to close a deal, only to ignore those rules themselves, and even do so blatantly. They forget the message they are sending here to others, which the rules are meaningless, do whatever you want.

Rules keep the company running effectively for the long term. Everyone should follow them.

34.

"LEARN TO SAY...I DON'T KNOW."

Too often New Entrepreneurs feel compelled to know everything, or at least pretend they do in front of clients, employees and investors. But it's BS, and experienced business people, and people in general, will know it for what it is. Pretension here ruins an opportunity to learn, grow and find out areas of interest and areas where improvement is needed.

So it's essential that new Entrepreneurs, and even old ones too, get comfortable saying the words, "I don't know." No one is expecting you to know absolutely everything, every option, contingency, nuanced element. It's ok. Acknowledge it, be honest about it, then if it's truly an important aspect, get busy researching and thinking through the correct answer to it.

35.

"DON'T GET CAUGHT UP IN THE LATEST BUSINESS JARGON."

The Business industry produces new jargon, new cliches and new by-words every year like weeds and most come and go like the seasons. It's important to not get too caught up and dance yourself into circles like a dog chasing its tail because the latest greatest idea ever about measuring your business is sweeping the articles on social media.

Focus on the classic themes and advice that have stood the test of time. They will lead you to better results over time as they will focus you on key metrics that work across industries and business types.

Remember: Sales, Gross Margin and Profitability never go out of style.

36.

"MAKE A SLOW TRANSISTION FROM DOING TO MANAGING."

This is the toughest evolution for managers of new businesses. Most businesses start with either one-person or a team together that handle almost all of the core activities of a new company. The addition of a first employee, or even part-time consultants, represents a milestone in the company while often creating problems for the Entrepreneur.

The key is going slow here. Too often owners rush this, not giving enough time to develop a productive management style. Sometimes they try to be everybody's best friend, sometimes they act like a perfectionist tyrant. Neither are beneficial. Slow down, do research, study and learn.

37.

"MAKE CRITICAL INVESTMENTS IN YOURSELF & THE COMPANY."

If you're a beginner entrepreneur, someone who didn't study business, you need to increase your skills, knowledge and experience. It's okay to be insufficient at inception, but staying that way is unacceptable. Make critical investments in yourself and the business to upgrade You. Too often new entrepreneurs don't find the money or the time.

Examples: Online or in-person business classes, industry-specific trade magazine subscriptions, industry networking conferences. There are thousands of ideas and opportunities. Invest.

And yes, please please please, take vacation! Health, both physical and mental, matter in success.

38.

"LEAN. PUSH. SHOVE."

Getting things achieved in a business is difficult and often demands some level of conflict. Weather in discussions with clients or in internal relations with employees, we need to recognise the use of metaphorical Force in getting things done. I always suggest graduated increases in pressure that I call Lean Push Shove.

I a perfect world we use just the right amount of force necessary to get done what we need accomplished. First we apply very moderate pressure which I call lean. San Juan necessary we apply more which I think of as pushing someone. When all else fails, sometimes, we do need to resort to shoving.

Learning to gradually increase pressure is a valuable skill.

39.

"UNDERSTAND THAT PEOPLE WON'T TELL YOU THE TRUTH."

This is the way the world works, and it is even more so the truth in business. People aren't honest especially when delivering bad news. We have to recognize that most people will avoid telling us bad things and we have to factor this fact into assumptions we are making about our business.

Be it employees, suppliers or our customers, conflict avoidance especially when there is something valued to be lost, will drive false communication.

It is incumbent on the entrepreneur to push and probe further to ensure they've gotten honest answers for things that have and have an occurred. then do something useful with the hard-won honesty gained.

40.

"COUNTERPARTIES WILL TAKE EVERY INCH THEY CAN GET."

Don't be angry about this, that's their job. Their job is to get anything and everything they can, within of course, all legal means. This is business, it is not necessarily some fair, well-meaning charitable endeavor. If you give someone you're dealing with an opportunity to take advantage of a situation you should plan on the fact that they will.

Most businesses are struggling to succeed, or at a minimum, struggling to succeed more. Just like you and yours. So it is incumbent on a business person to do their job to the fullest, acting with thoroughness and professionalism to ensure you have gotten what you deserve.

41.

"BELIEVE IN AND USE THE K.I.S.S. METHOD."

K.I.S.S. = Keep It Simple, Stupid. Nine times out of 10 the simplest approach will be the most effective. Ranging across a business organization from implementing sales programs to building products to managing inventories to tracking accounting entries, especially with small businesses, one should strive to keep processes simple for them to have the greatest possible chance for success.

Success in so many areas of a Small Business depends on intricate element working in unison. Complexity creates opportunities for disconnect and breakdowns. If something isn't working, often the answer is to find ways make it simpler.

42.

"NO BAD SURPRISES
TO ANYONE. EVER!"

While in life certain surprises can be a wonderful thing, in Business, surprises are failures and all must endeavor not to surprise. Whether it be employees or clients or the postman, the job of managers on major issues is not to surprise the people you're working with.

Not only does it represent poor management skills, but additionally it puts at risk the trust that has been built up between two sides in a relationship. It is this trust that often undergirds successful business relationships, and its loss through surprising someone can have long-term detrimental effects.

Avoiding surprises demands respectful communication skills far enough in advance so that appropriate planning can occur.

43.

"IF YOU'RE NON-CONFRONTATIONAL, GET SOMEONE TO DO YOUR CONFLICT."

Conflict is an undeniable, and even essential element of business. At some point and usually at many points often, it will be necessary to fight for your ideas, for your products, for your company. That's the Business world, like it or not.

If you do not yet have the capacity to handle conflict and confrontations, it is important for the company to engage someone who can handle that role for the company. The key will be doing engage someone who you can learn from and who ultimately you can replace when you have developed the necessary tools to handle conflict in an appropriate manner that will protect your company and your investments.

44.

"BE HESITANT ABOUT QUICK SOLUTIONS."

The Hippocratic oath's second principal is the one of non-malfeasence. It counsels doctors when dealing with patients, To First, Do No Harm. It is a reminder to all that sometimes the right decision is to not do anythin. Because often enough, when not well-analyzed or thought out, the solution ends up worse than the problem.

It is especially true when the allure of quick solutions raise their spectre. Business problems are tough, and often intractable, and it is rarely the first suggestion that ends up being the right solution. There is a natural inclination in business people to wish problems away in order to focus on more pleasant things. One must fight that inclination.

181

45.

"SPEND MORE TIME ON HIRING THAN YOU THINK NECESSARY."

While waiting for the perfect hire is an endless empty pursuit, a company in the end is its employees and bad hires can have a tremendous detrimental effect short and long-term. Even greater than the benefit of good hires, the cost of bad hires is registered internally and externally and is difficult and costly to overcome.

So take the time, invest in a hiring process that both weeds out bad apples and find true good-fits for the position and the organization as a whole. This means doing second and even third interviews, if necessary. This means having multiple different people interview a candidate so a consensus can be built. It eve n potentially means background checks and thorough conversations with referrals provided.

46.

"SMALL BUSINESSES MUST USE TECHNOLOGY TO LEVERAGE EFFORTS & ACTIVITIES."

It is so hard when you are a one two or three person business to complete well all the tasks and activities necessary to grow a successful business. In many ways it's almost impossible to achieve that without the latest technology to multiply your efforts.

However, so much software exists, even free software, to automate and leverage your efforts. Be it Google, Microsoft, Adobe, and even much smaller companies suite of products and programs, be agnostic to the provider, be a follower to the productivity gains.

Follow some technology influencers to capitalize on latest innovations in time-saving programs, products.

THANK YOUS & ACKNOWLEDGEMENTS

I would like to thank enormously the following, which helped make this endeavor possible and cost effective:

CANVA SOFTWARE: This is an incredible software program and application that allows one to build graphic projects such as this book. The paid-tier is even better as it allows you a ton of free photos for use.

PIXABAY: This is a magnificent site that allows you to download free photos for use in products such as this e-book.

Thank you to my editor, Richard Putterman.

Thank you to my many clients over the years, who have been the sounding board and on the receiving end of these "Tips" as I created and refined them.

ABOUT THE PUBLISHER:
GOLDART PUBLISHING LLC

Goldart Publishing LLC is a sister company of Goldart Consulting LLC is a Small Business Consulting practice specializing in Finance, Marketing, Strategic Planning and Management. It was started 22 years ago with the goal of bringing the latest in Enterprise advisory, the skills, practices and efforts oftentimes the difference between success and failure, to Small Businesses companies at a cost that is not prohibitive. Over these years, we have helped countless Enterprises in myriad industries and countries accomplish the goals they've set out to achieve.

At Goldart, we use a holistic approach, recognizing all the Essential elements necessary for Small Business success. These core aspects make meaningful impact on companies. Together with our group of Corporate partners, we offer counseling, expertise and hands-on output designed to drive revenue, profitability and long-term financial stability and success."

Please feel free to contact us if you need help with your Small or Mid-sized Business

Goldart Consulting LLC
(888) 203 -6419
www.goldartcconsulting.com

Made in United States
Troutdale, OR
12/28/2023